IMPRESSIONS of

CYPRUS

Produced by AA Publishing

Published by AA Publishing (a trading name of Automobile Association Developments Limited, whose registered office is Fanum House, Basing View, Basingstoke, Hampshire RG21 4EA; registered number 1878835)

ISBN: 978-0-7495-5858-1

A03676

A CIP catalogue record for this book is available from the British Library.

Colour reproduction by KDP, Kingsclere
Printed and bound in China by C & C Offset Printing Co. Ltd

Opposite: A view across the village of Lefkara, in the Larnaca district. The village is famed for its lacemaking.

IMPRESSIONS of

CYPRUS

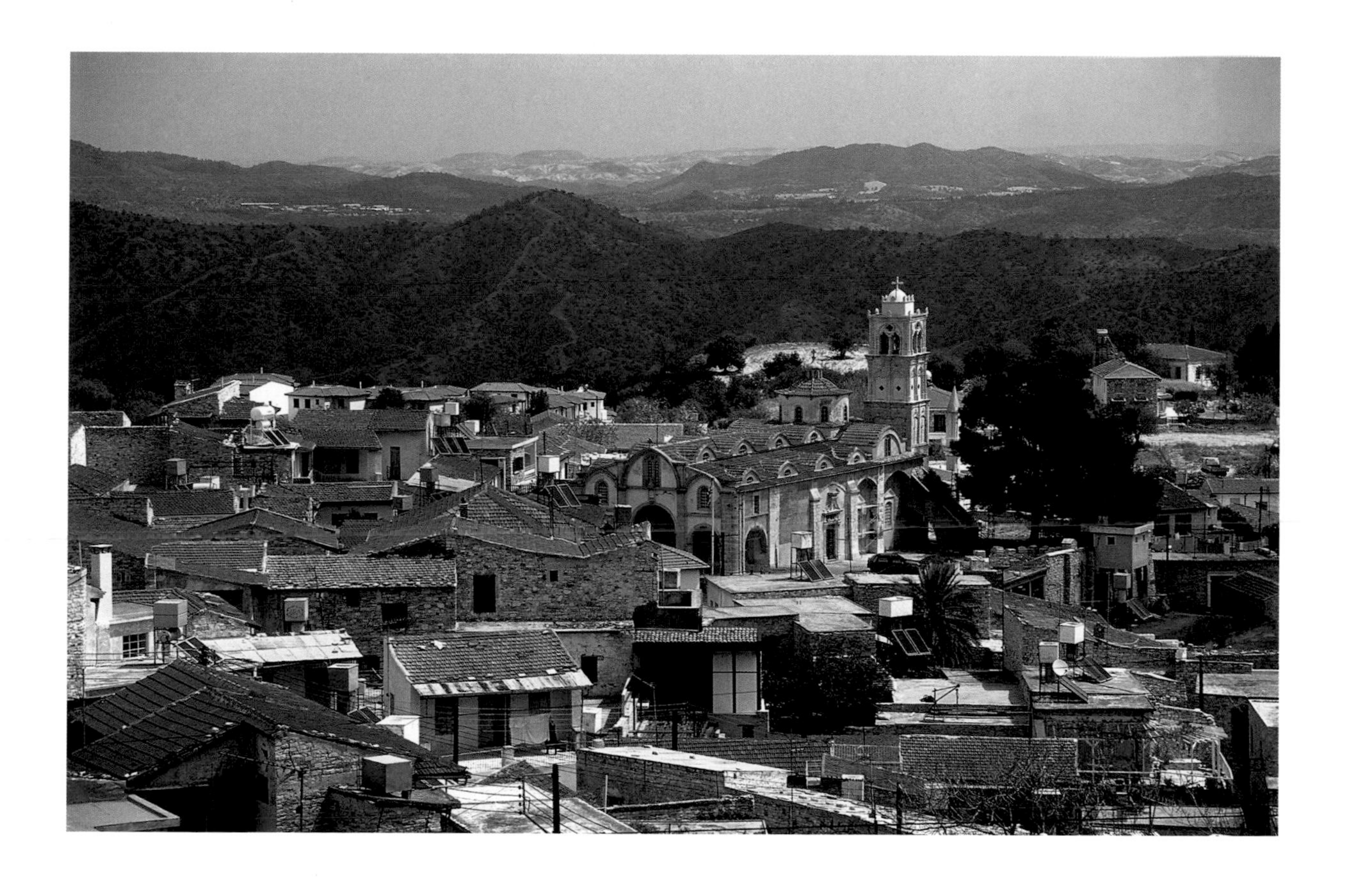

Picture Acknowledgements

The Automobile Association would like to thank the following photographers, companies and picture libraries for their assistance in the preparation of this book.

Abbreviations for the picture credits are as follows: (t) top; (b) bottom; (l) left; (r) right; (AA) AA World Travel Library.

Front Cover AA/M Birkitt; Back Cover AA/A Kouprianoff; Back Cover inset AA/M Birkitt;

3 AA/S Day; 5 AA/S Day; 7 AA/A Kouprianoff; 8 AA/A Kouprianoff; 9 AA/A Kouprianoff; 10 AA/M Birkitt; 11 Alamy/Rainer Jahns; 12 AA/M Birkitt; 13 AA/S Day; 14 AA/R Rainford; 15 AA/A Kouprianoff; 16 AA/A Kouprianoff; 17 AA/S Day; 18 AA/A Kouprianoff; 19 AA/S Day; 20 AA/A Kouprianoff; 21 AA/R Rainford; 22 AA/M Birkitt; 23 AA/S Day; 24 AA/S Day; 25 AA/S Day; 26 AA/M Birkitt; 27 AA/M Birkitt; 28 AA/A Kouprianoff; 29 AA/M Birkitt; 30 AA/S Day; 31 AA/A Kouprianoff; 32 AA/S Day; 33 AA/A Kouprianoff; 34 AA/S Day; 35 AA/S Day; 36 AA/A Kouprianoff; 37 AA/A Kouprianoff; 38 AA/A Kouprianoff; 39 AA/M Birkitt; 40 AA/A Kouprianoff; 41 AA/S Day; 42 AA/A Kouprianoff; 43 AA/S Day; 44 AA/A Kouprianoff; 45 AA/S Day; 46 AA/A Kouprianoff; 47 AA/R Rainford; 48 AA/A Kouprianoff; 49 AA/S Day; 50 AA/M Birkitt; 51 AA/M Birkitt; 52 AA/R Rainford; 53 AA/A Kouprianoff; 54 AA/A Kouprianoff; 55 AA/S Day; 56 AA/A Kouprianoff; 57 AA/A Kouprianoff; 58 AA/A Kouprianoff; 59 Alamy/Dave Watts; 60 AA/A Kouprianoff; 61 AA/R Rainford; 62 AA/A Kouprianoff; 63 AA/M Birkitt; 64 AA/S Day; 65 AA/S Day; 66 AA/S Day; 67 AA/S Day; 68 AA/M Birkitt; 69 AA/A Kouprianoff; 70 AA/M Birkitt; 71 AA/S Day; 72 AA/A Kouprianoff; 73 AA/A Kouprianoff; 74 Alamy/Jim Nicholson; 75 AA/A Kouprianoff; 76 AA/A Kouprianoff; 77 AA/A Kouprianoff; 78 AA/A Kouprianoff; 79 AA/A Kouprianoff; 80 AA/R Rainford; 81 AA/A Kouprianoff; 82 AA/S Day; 83 AA/S Day; 84 AA/S Day; 85 AA/S Day; 86 AA/M Birkitt; 87 AA/S Day; 88 AA/A Kouprianoff; 89 AA/S Day; 90 AA/M Birkitt; 91 AA/R Rainford; 92 AA/A Kouprianoff; 93 AA/S Day; 94 AA/S Day; 95 AA/S Day

Every effort has been made to trace the copyright holders, and we apologise in advance for any accidental errors. We would be happy to apply the corrections in the following edition of this publication.

Opposite: Looking across the Xeros Potamos Valley.

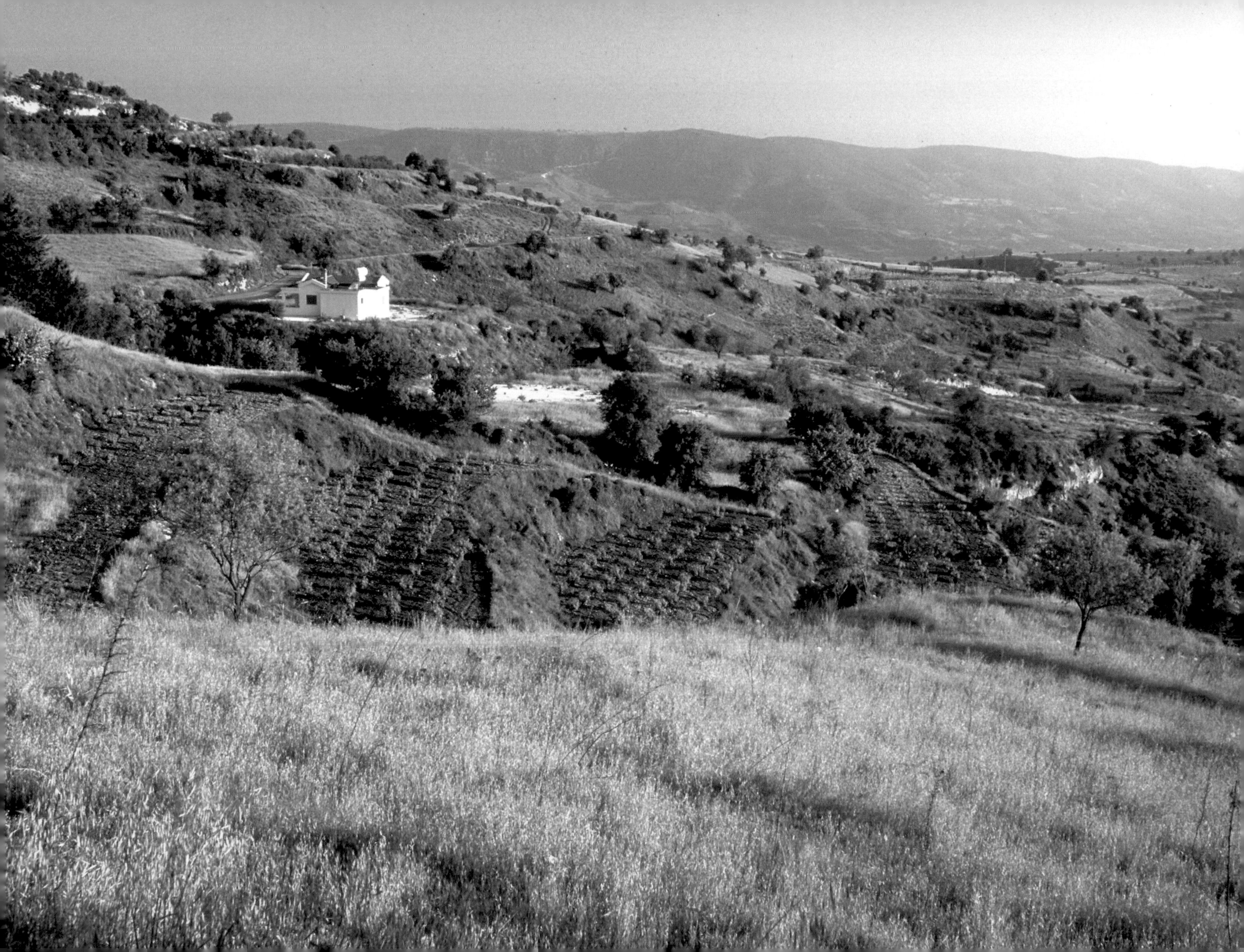

INTRODUCTION

Cyprus is a jewel in the Mediterranean Sea, a prize that has been fought over by powerful nations throughout history. The island was inhabited in the Stone Age and still displays the remains of villages from the time when agriculture arrived there. Greeks first settled on the island around 1600 BC. Phoenicians, Egyptians, Persians, Romans, Byzantines and Venetians were among the many settlers who followed. In the 16th century the Ottoman Empire of nearby Turkey conquered the island and held it for over 300 years. The Turks infused their own Muslim culture into its Greek culture, and then lost control of the island to Britain in 1878. Only on 16th August 1960 did Cyprus at last gain independence.

Now Cyprus, the third largest island in the Mediterranean, is flourishing – thanks largely to the visitors who flock to it. They discover here an unparalleled diversity of natural and cultural wealth. Pleasure-seekers can bask on the beaches of Pafos and Limassol, or ski on the snows of Mount Olympos. They can drink ouzo and eat souvlaki (pork kebabs) in Greek tavernas. If they like night life they can party in the clubs and bars of Agia Napa. If they prefer outdoor pursuits they can hike along the forest trails of the Troodos massif, which dominates the centre of the island. Here they are assured of seeing a wealth of birdlife and if they are lucky they may also see the mouflon, the shy wild sheep of the region.

The human heritage of Cyprus is as rich as that of nature. There are Byzantine churches, simple on the outside, but with shadowy interiors made bright by frescoes. There are countless later churches in the Greek Orthodox style. Gothic churches can be found, too, from the time when the Franks ruled Cyprus. The Islamic stream in Cypriot culture is represented in the domes and minarets of numerous mosques.

Recent history casts a shadow over this richly favoured land. A military coup in 1974 aimed to unite the island with Greece, but this was forestalled by a Turkish invasion. Turkey occupied the northern third of the island, which later proclaimed itself the Turkish Republic of Northern Cyprus. Hundreds of thousands of Cypriots left homes that their forebears had occupied for generations, Greeks moving from the north to the south, Turks moving in the opposite direction. The United Nations still mans a buffer zone that snakes across the island and through the heart of the capital, Nicosia.

After decades of enforced peace, there are today tentative steps towards reconciliation of the two communities. Meanwhile over two million visitors come here every year to play hard and enjoy the island. According to the ancient fable, Aphrodite was born from the foam of the sea off Cyprus, and her cult inspired temples all across the island. The photographs collected here hint at why the island seemed such a fitting birthplace for the goddess of love and beauty.

Opposite: A trio of holidaymakers admire the view from Aphrodite's Rock, a rock formation which stands in shallow sea water at Pafos. The Rock has been regarded as the birthplace of Aphrodite since ancient times.

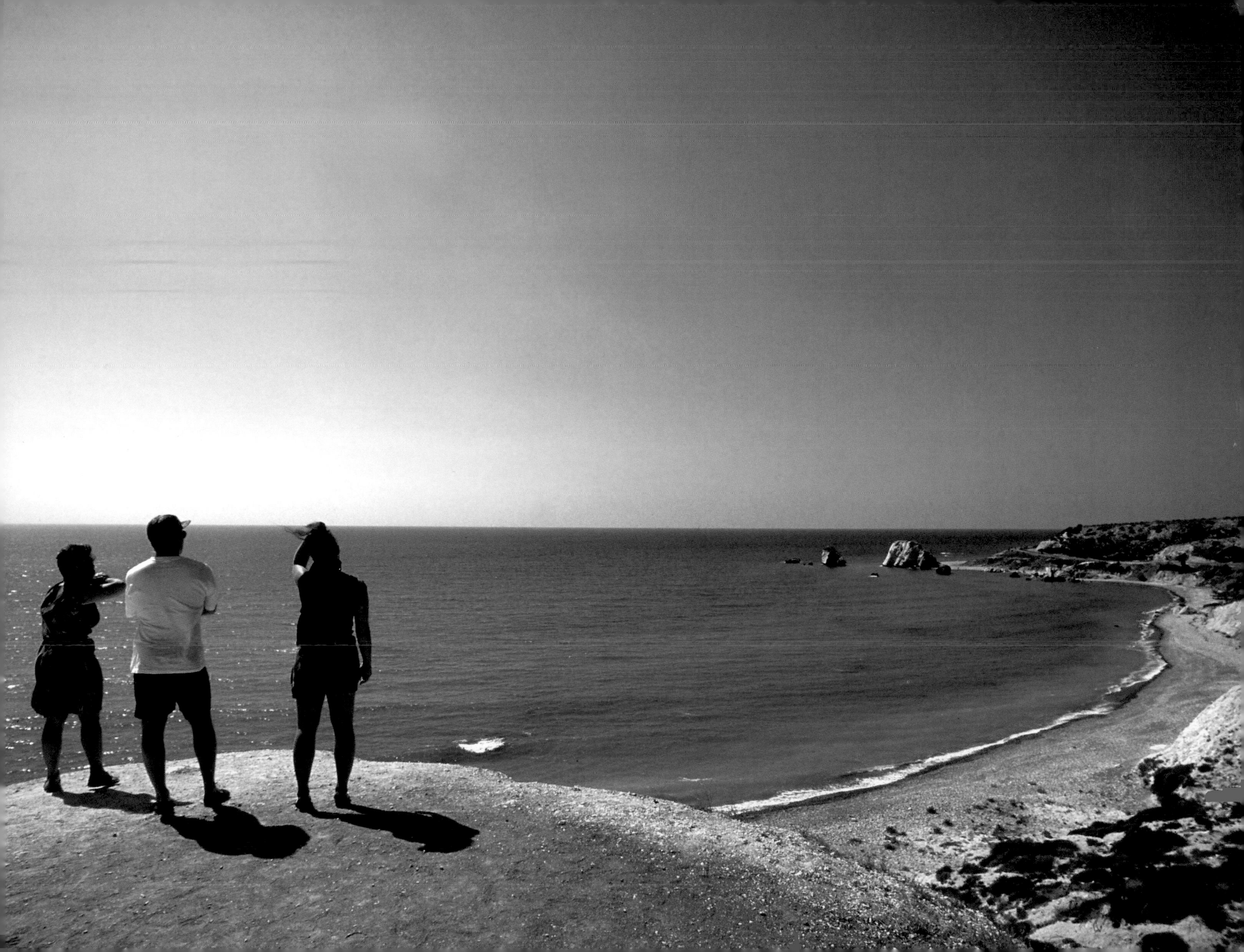

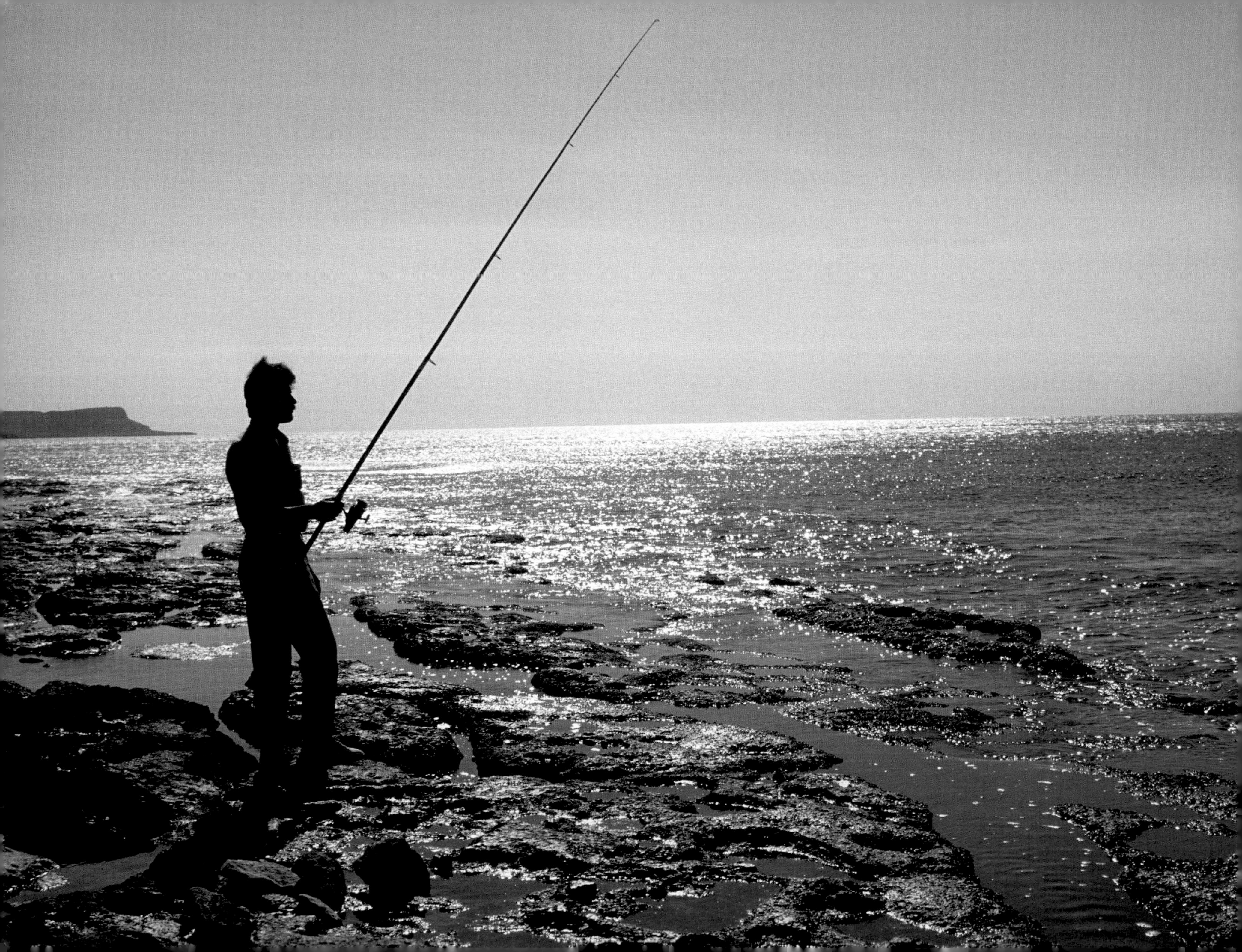

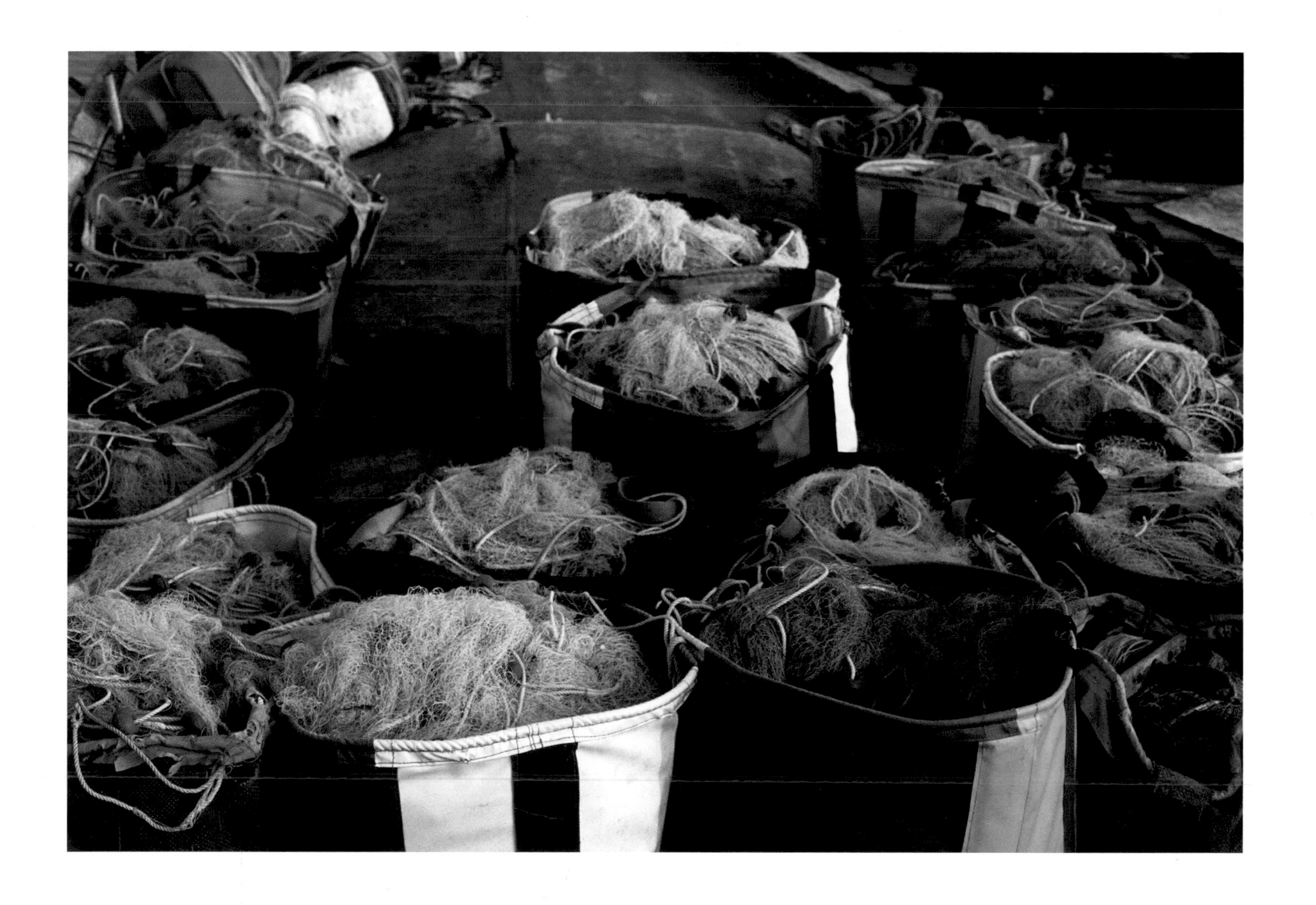

Striped bags hold nets on the deck of a fishing boat tied up in a Cyprus harbour.
Opposite: A sea angler fishes from the rocky coast near the resort of Agia Napa on the south-east coast of Cyprus, with sunlight glimmering on the blue waters of the Mediterranean.

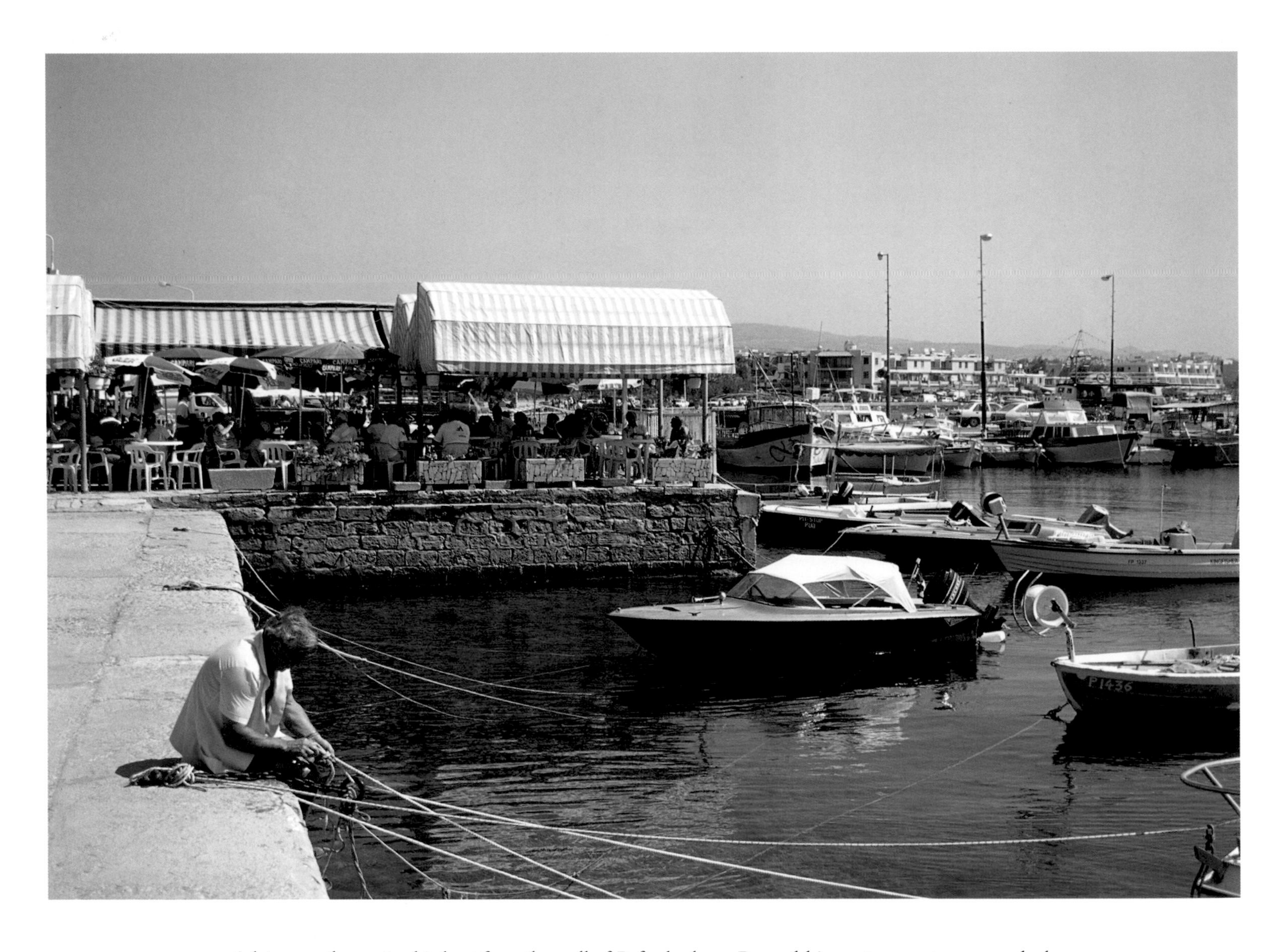

A leisure sailor unties his boat from the wall of Pafos harbour. Beyond him, a taverna terrace overlooks the fishing boats and pleasure craft that share the harbour.

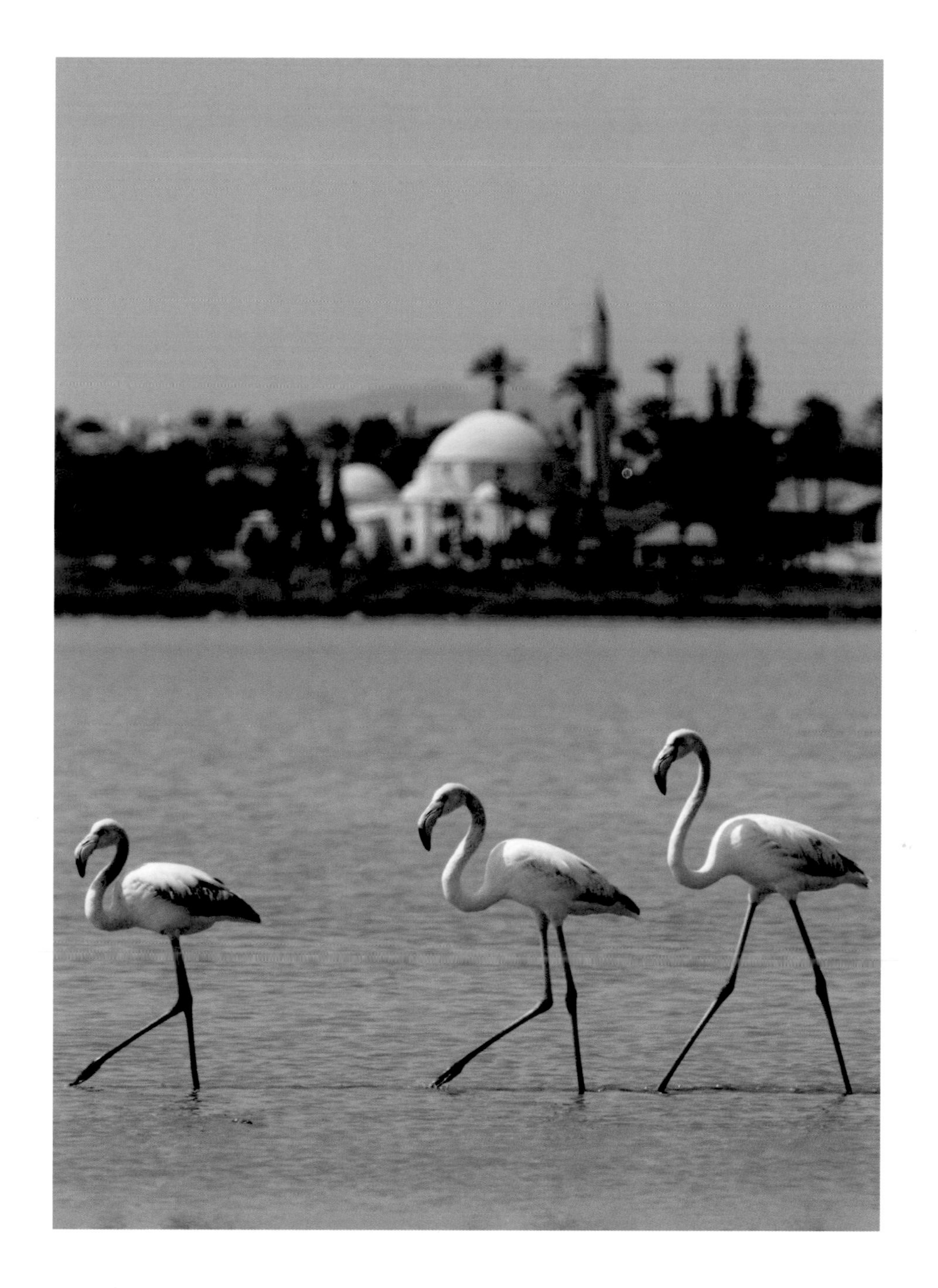

Flamingoes wade through a salt lake in front of Hala Sultan Tekkesi Mosque.

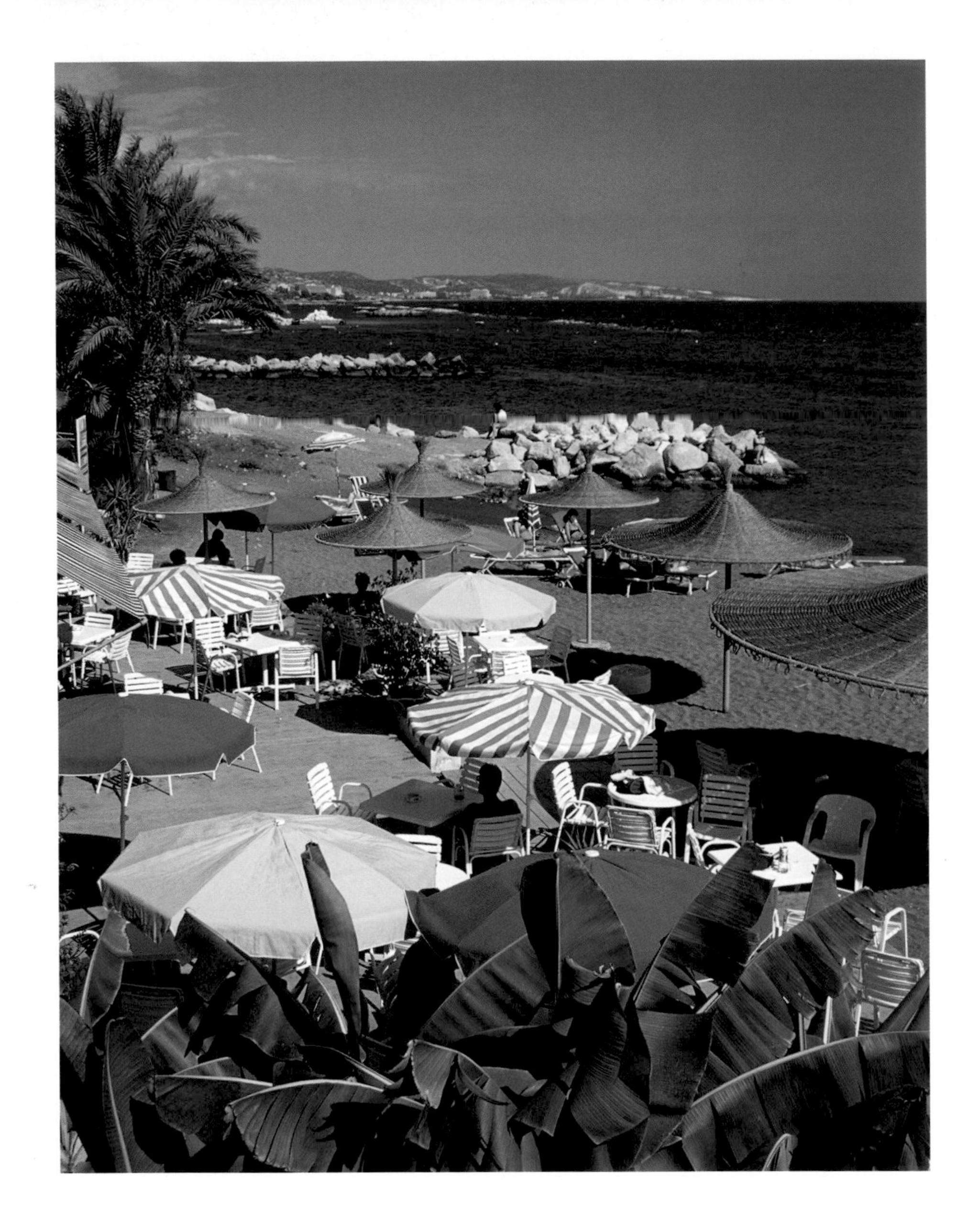

The brightly coloured umbrellas of a beach café cluster at the water's edge near Limassol, on Akrotin Bay.
Opposite: The coastline of the Akamas Peninsula.

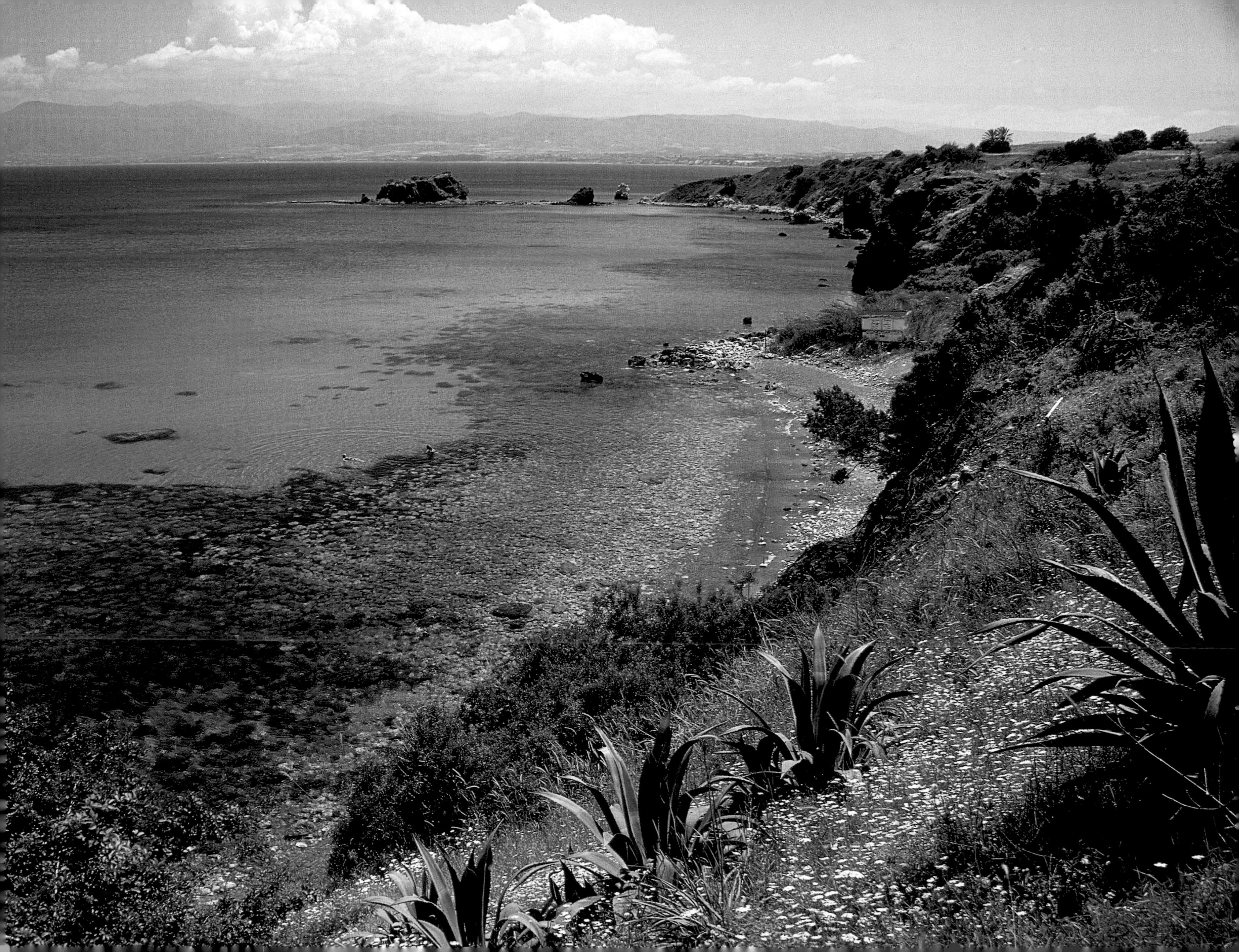

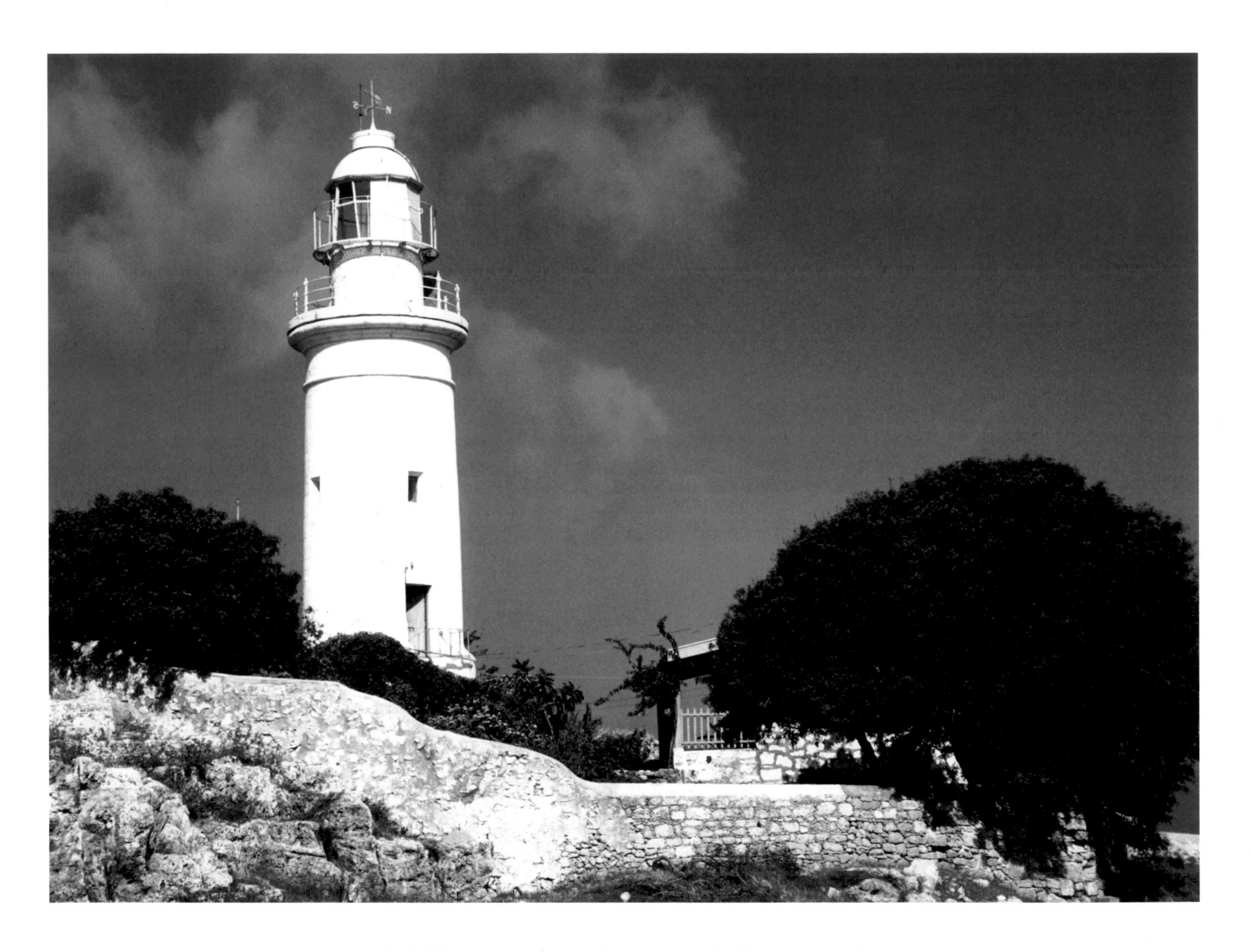

The lighthouse at Pafos stands out against the blue Cyprian sky.

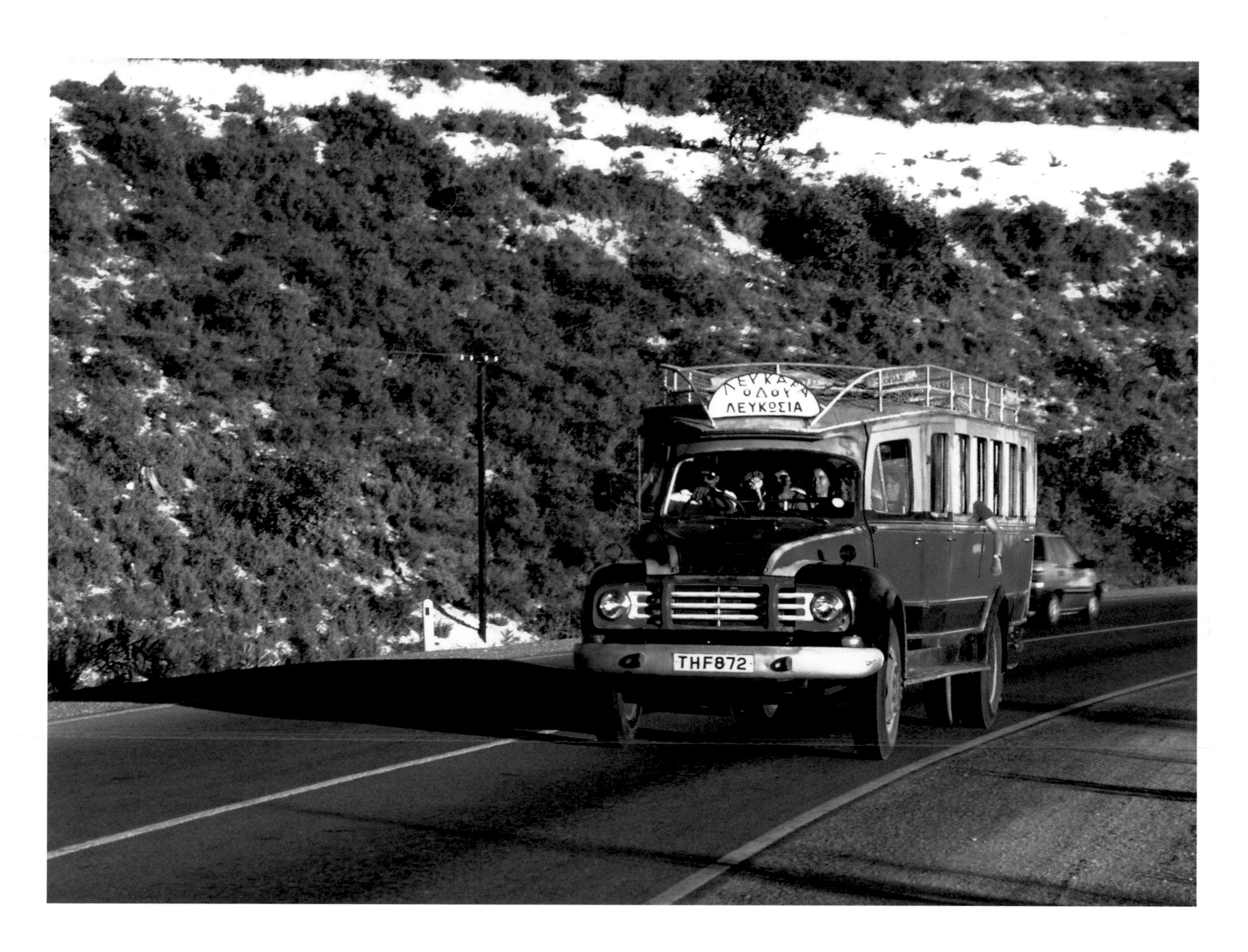

A packed local bus journeys in the vicinity of Lefkara in central southern Cyprus.

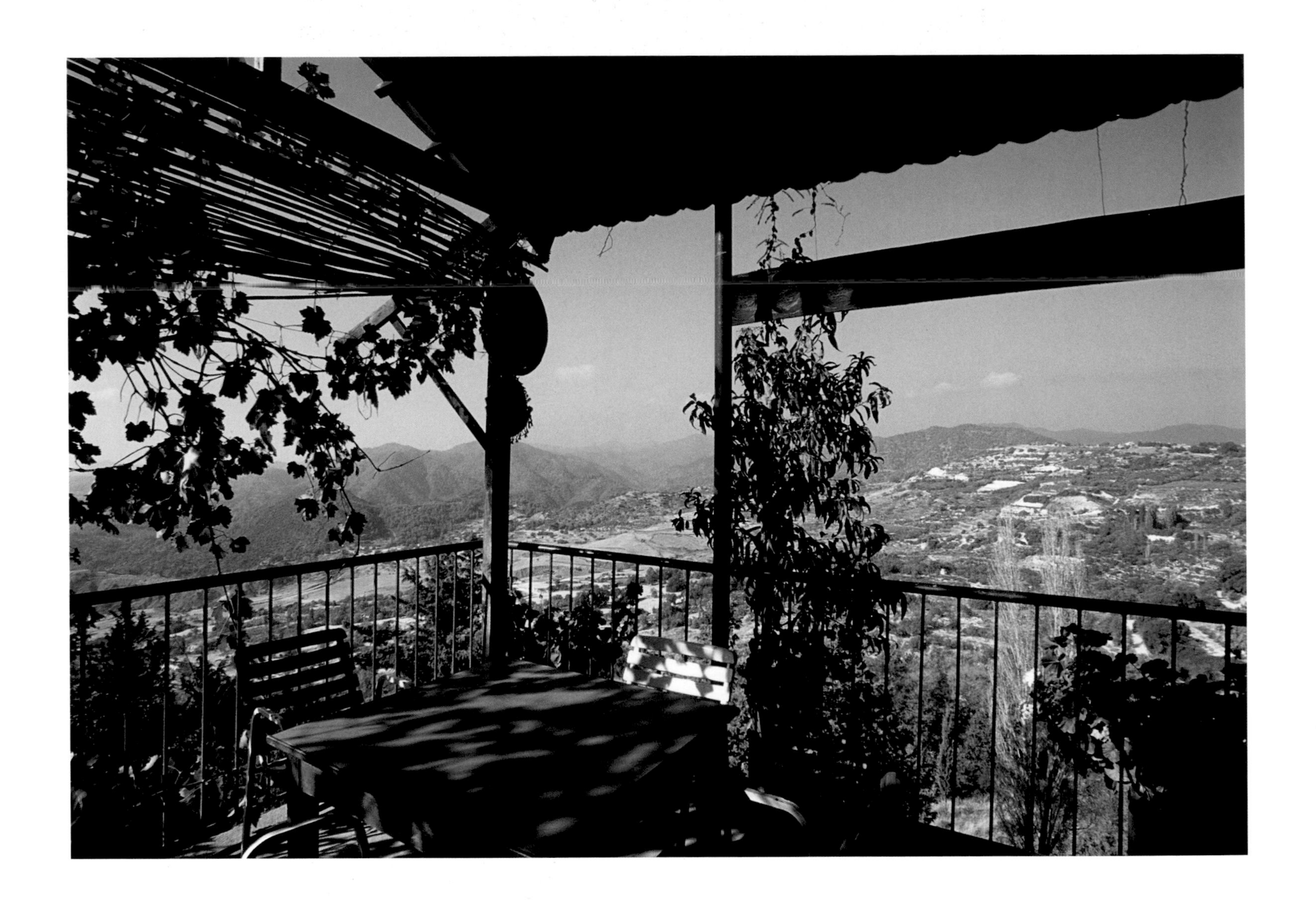

A flower-decked terrace at the Panagia Chrysorrogiatissa Monastery overlooks the forests and hills of the Paphos district.

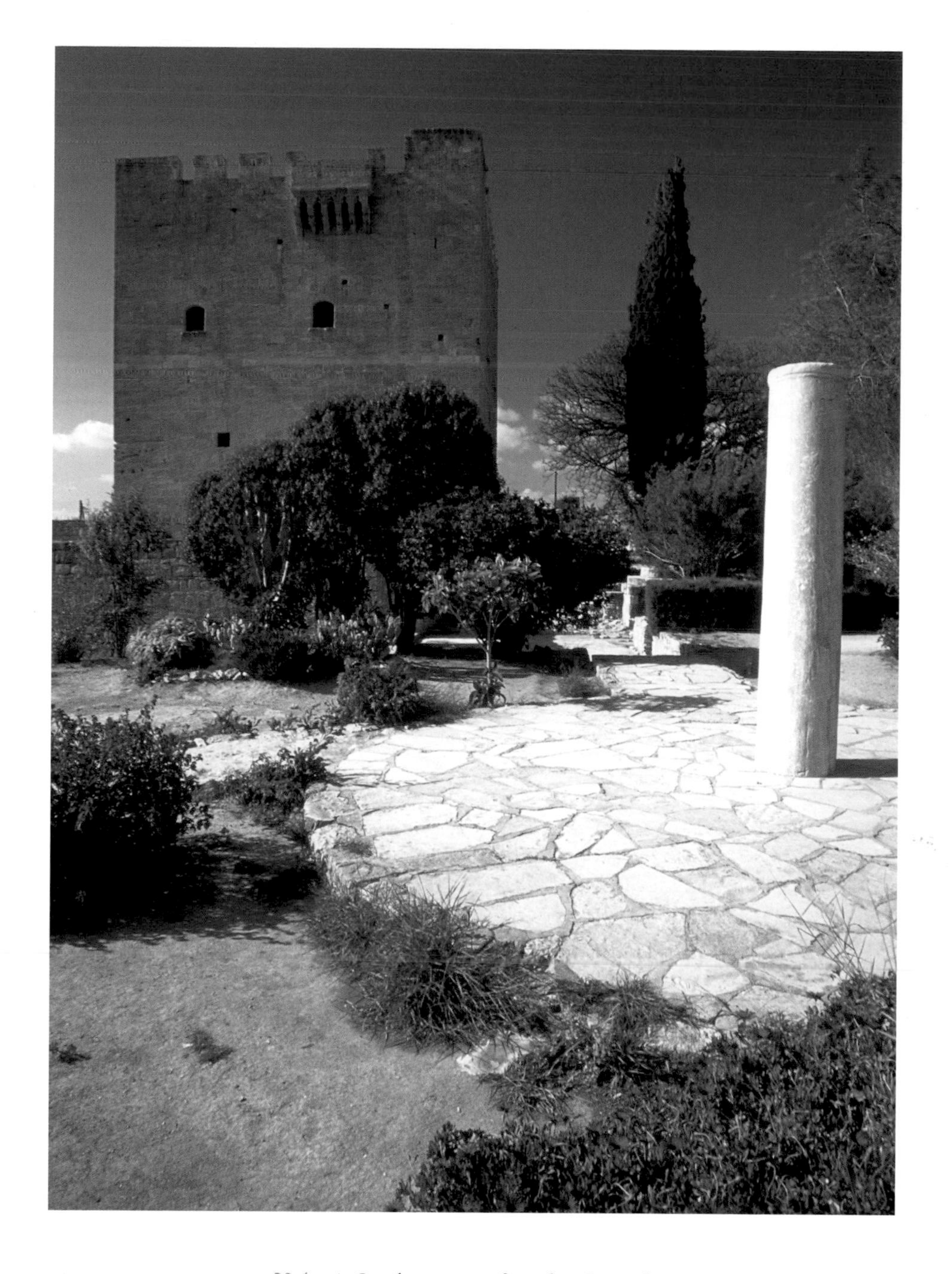

Kolossi Castle was a refuge for Crusaders
and today provides fine views from its battlements.

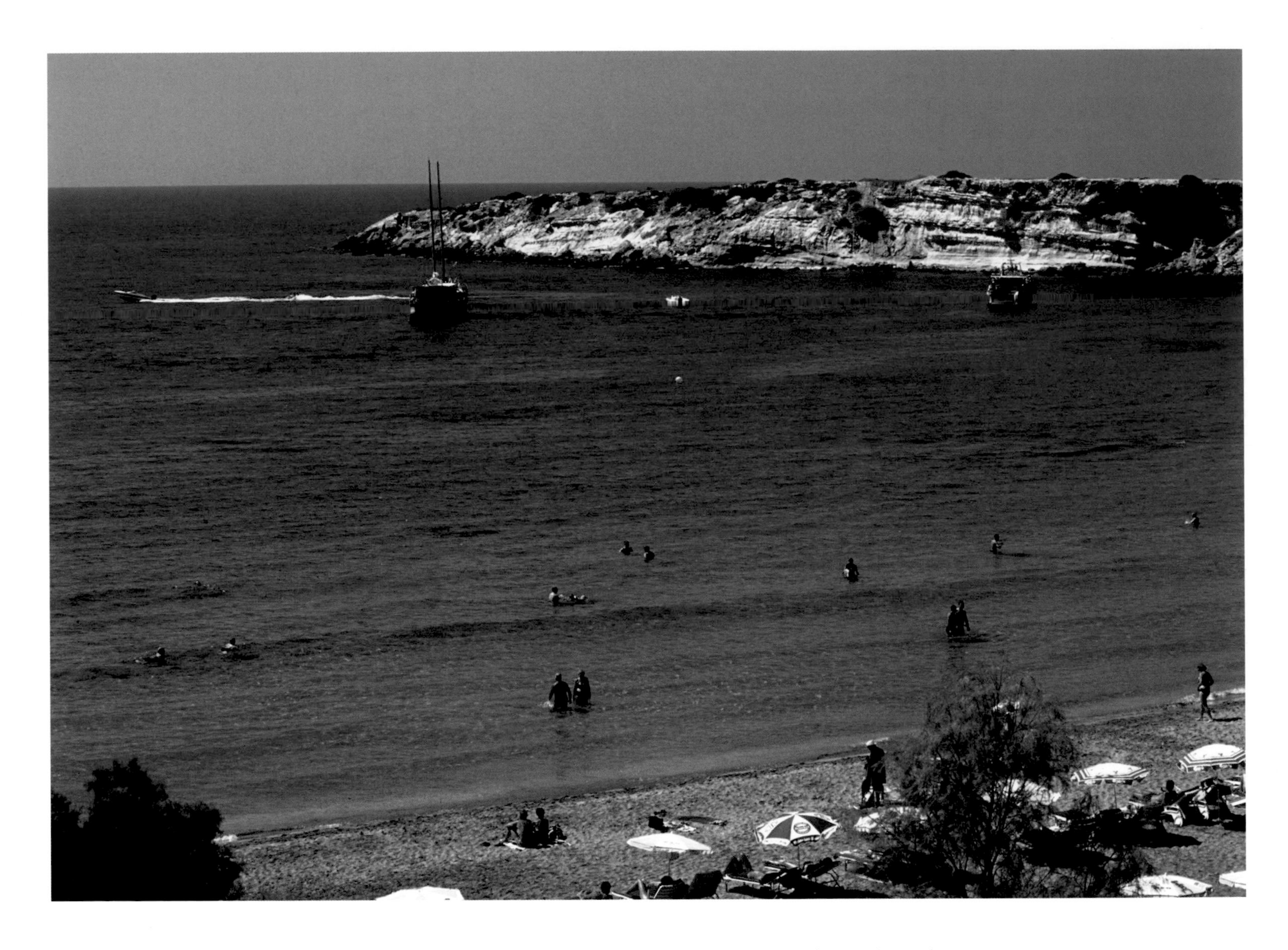

Sheltered by rock escarpments, Coral Bay is becoming increasingly popular with tourists.

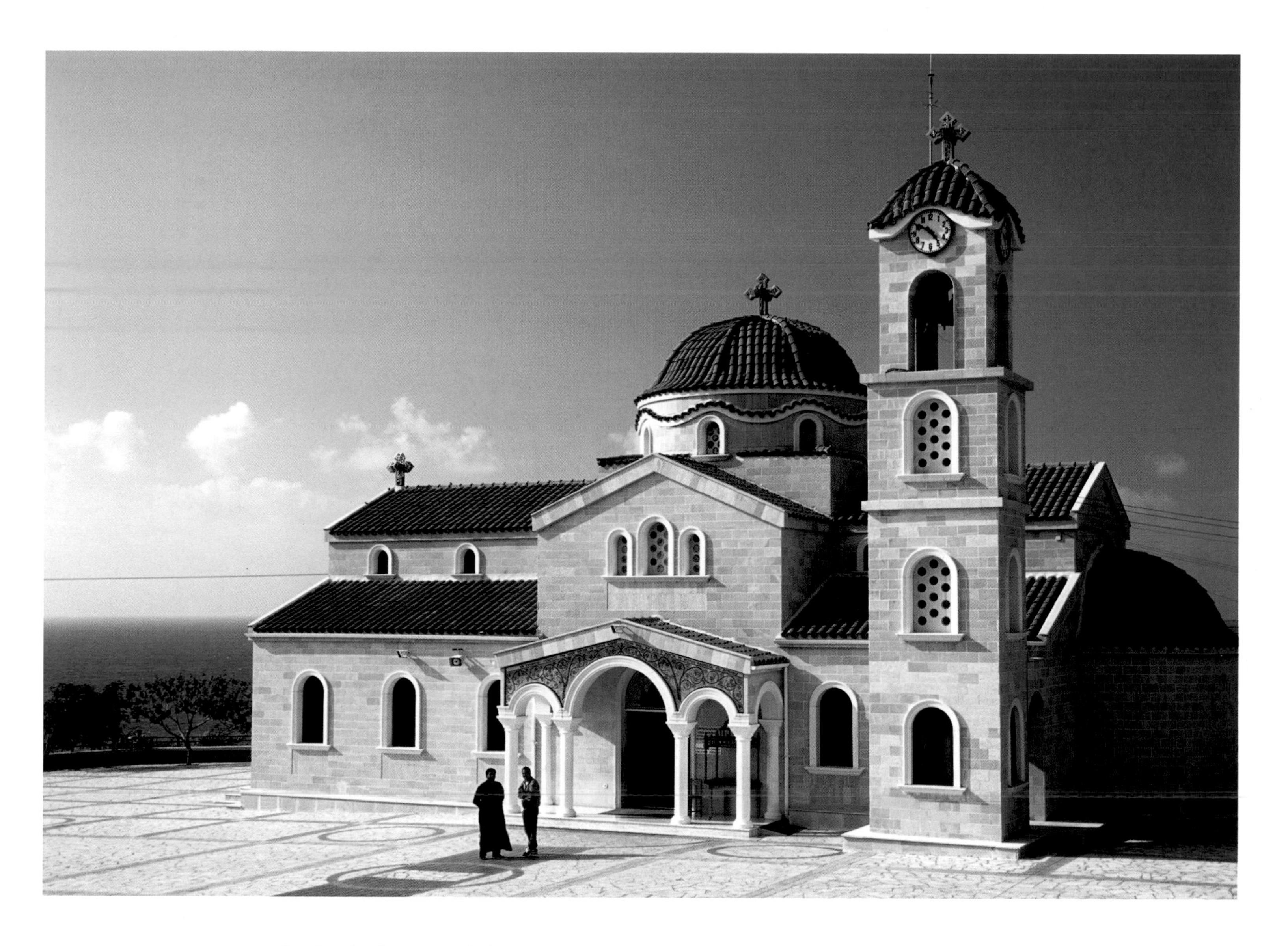

The church of Agios Rafaelis at Pachyammos on a headland overlooking the Mediterranean. The church, consecrated in 1992, is famous for the miraculous cures that take place there.

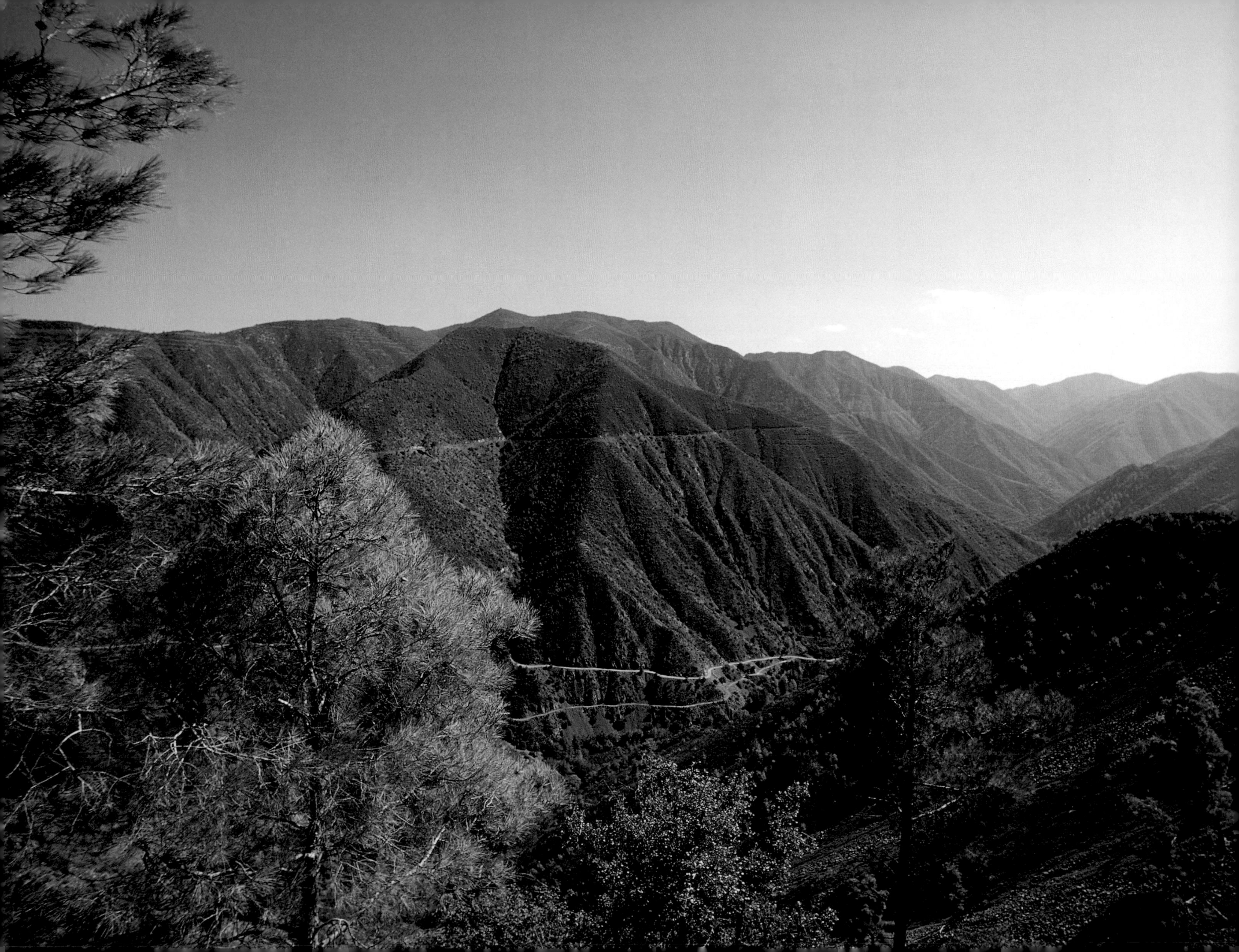

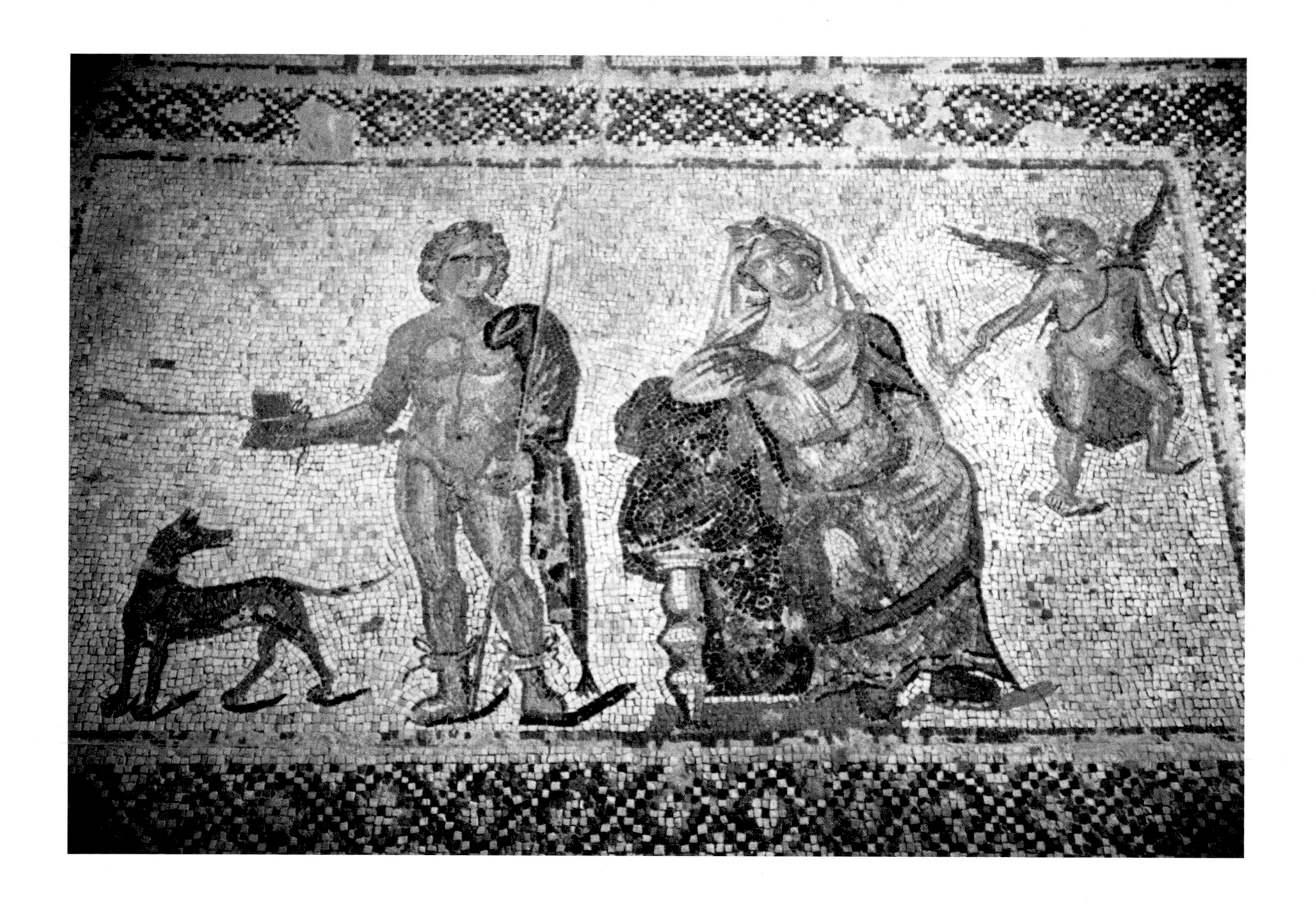

Detail of a mosaic floor in the House of Dionysos. The mosaics of Pafos were discovered in a cluster of buildings dating from the Roman period, principally the 3rd century AD.
Opposite: The dramatic lamdscape of Tillyria, in the Troodos foothills, stretches as far as the eye can see.

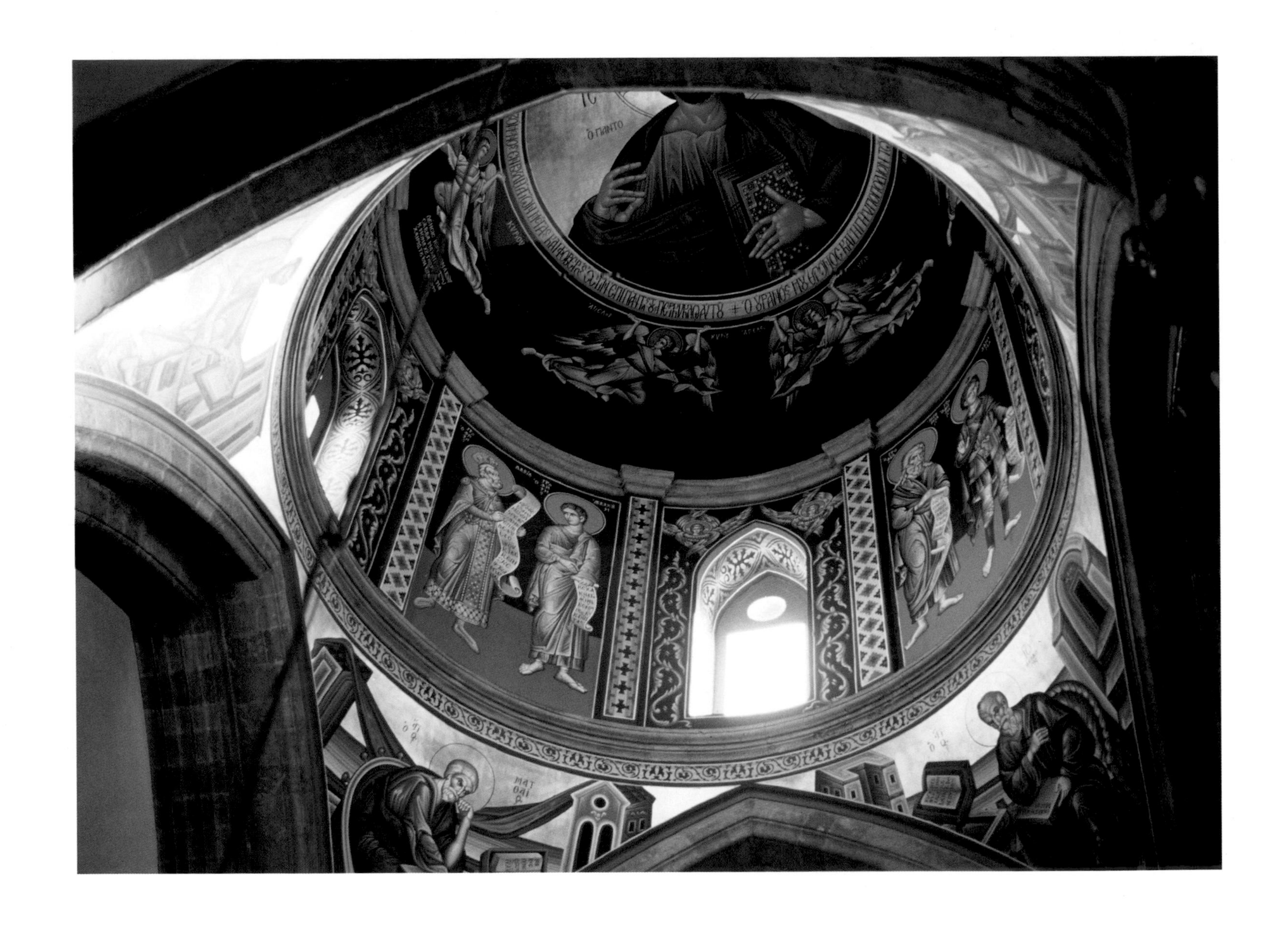

Modern panels decorate the interior of the church dome in the 19th-century Machairas Monastery, situated in the pinewoods of the mountains of the Nicosia district.

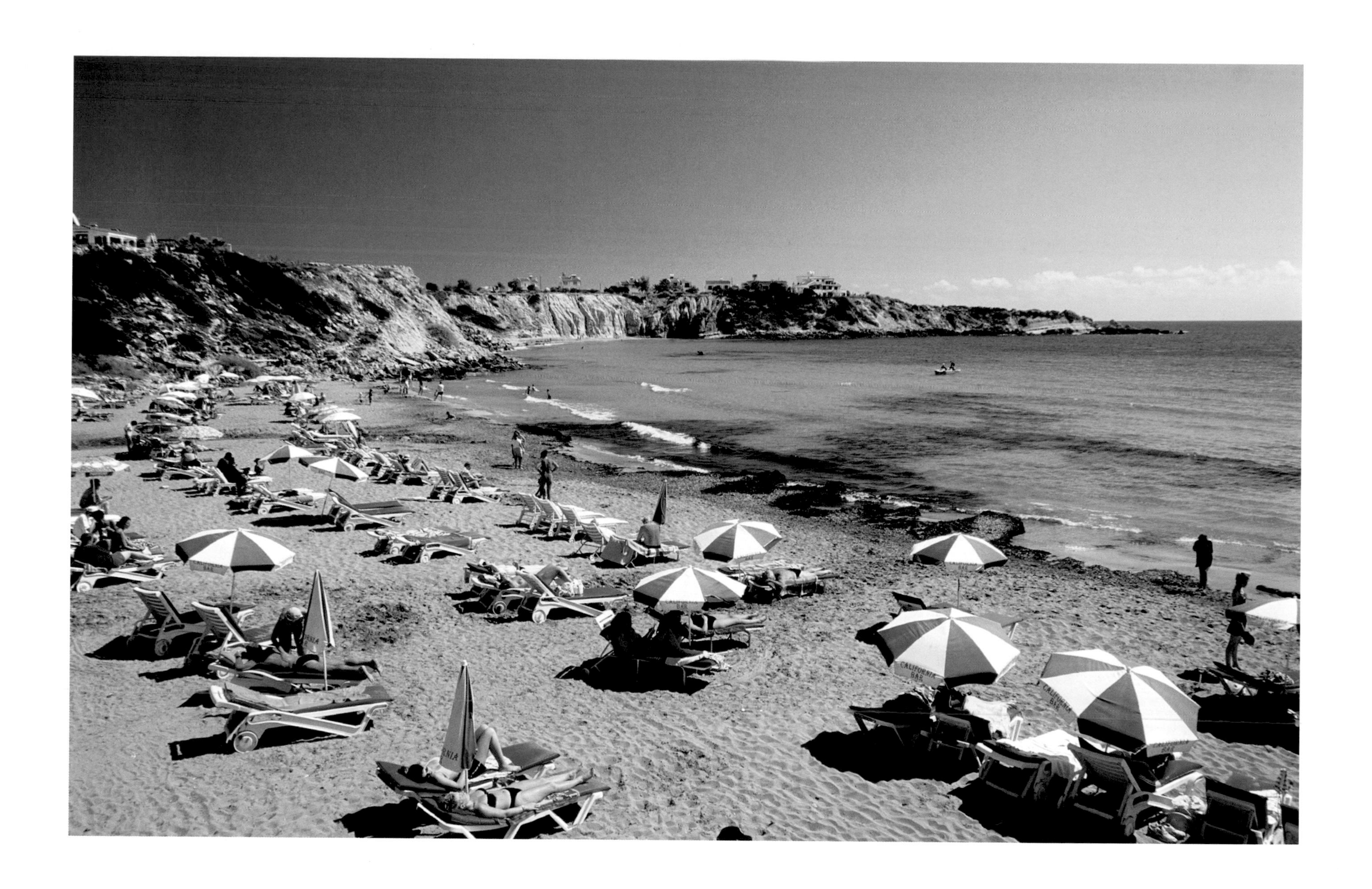

Holidaymakers enjoy the sandy beach at Coral Bay.

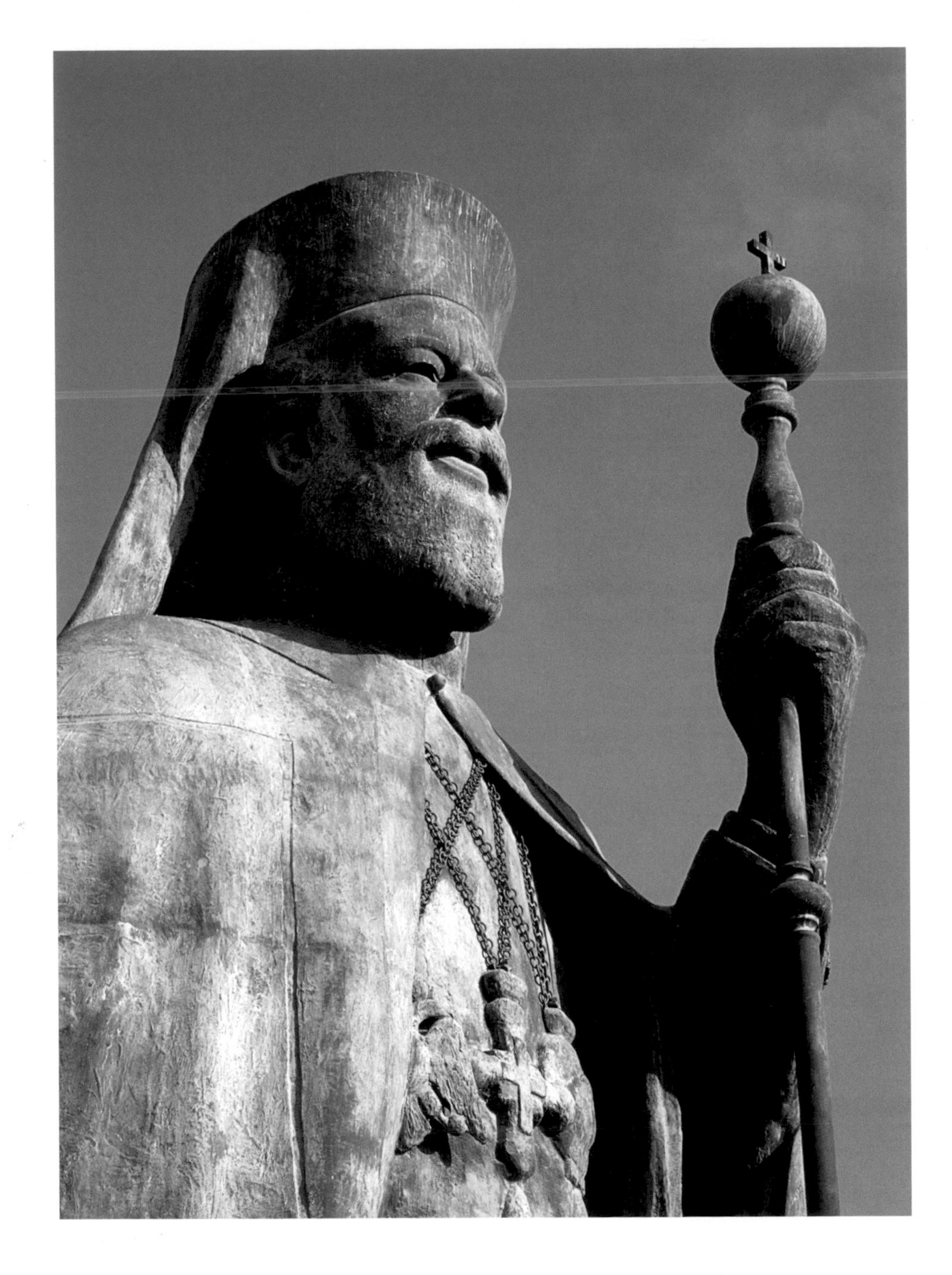

The statue of Archbishop Makarios who twice held the presidency of independent Cyprus, outside the Bishopric, Nicosia.

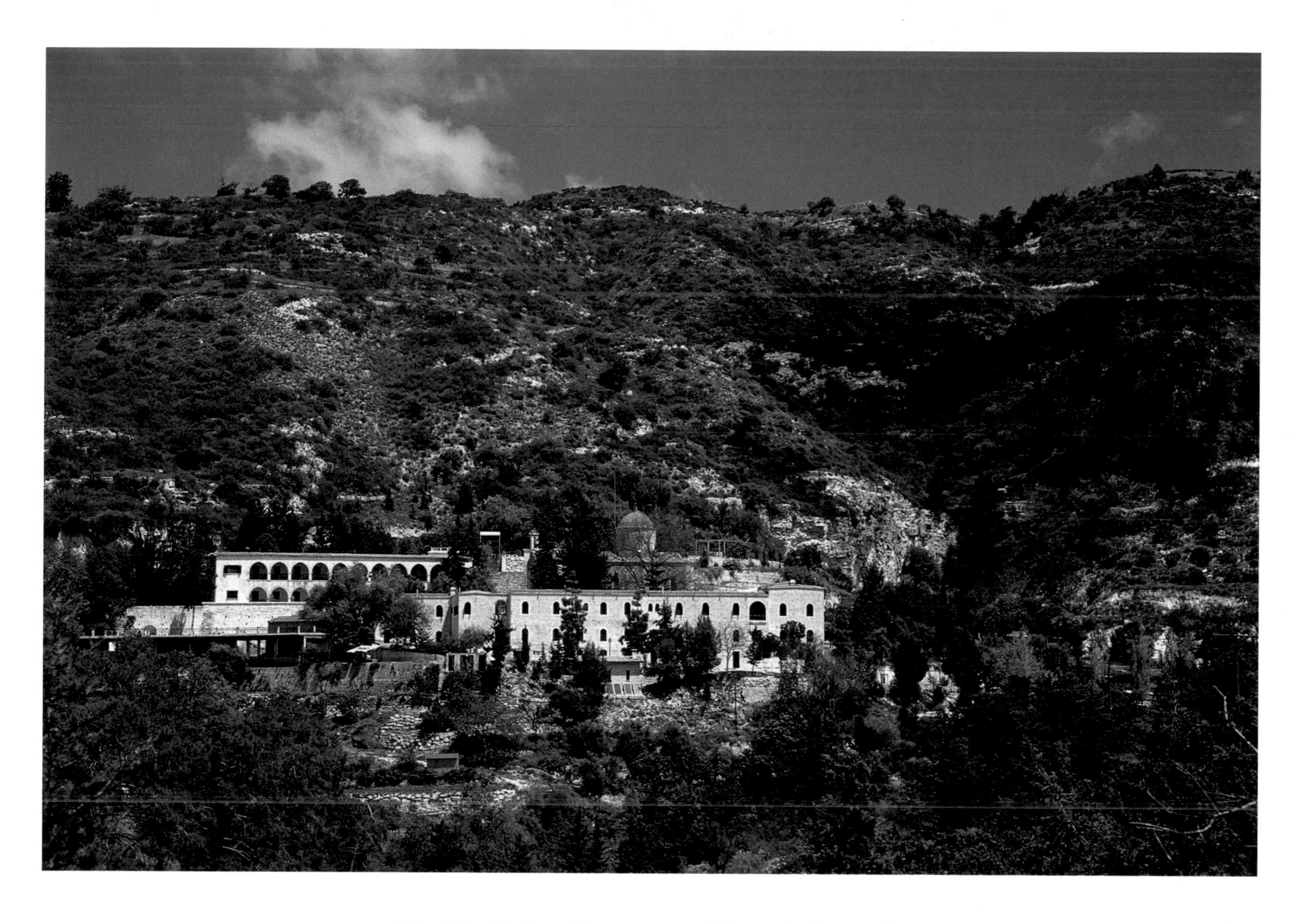

The Agios Neofytos Monastery near Tala, not far from Pafos.
The monastery was built on the site where Saint Neofytos found seclusion in caves in the 12th century.

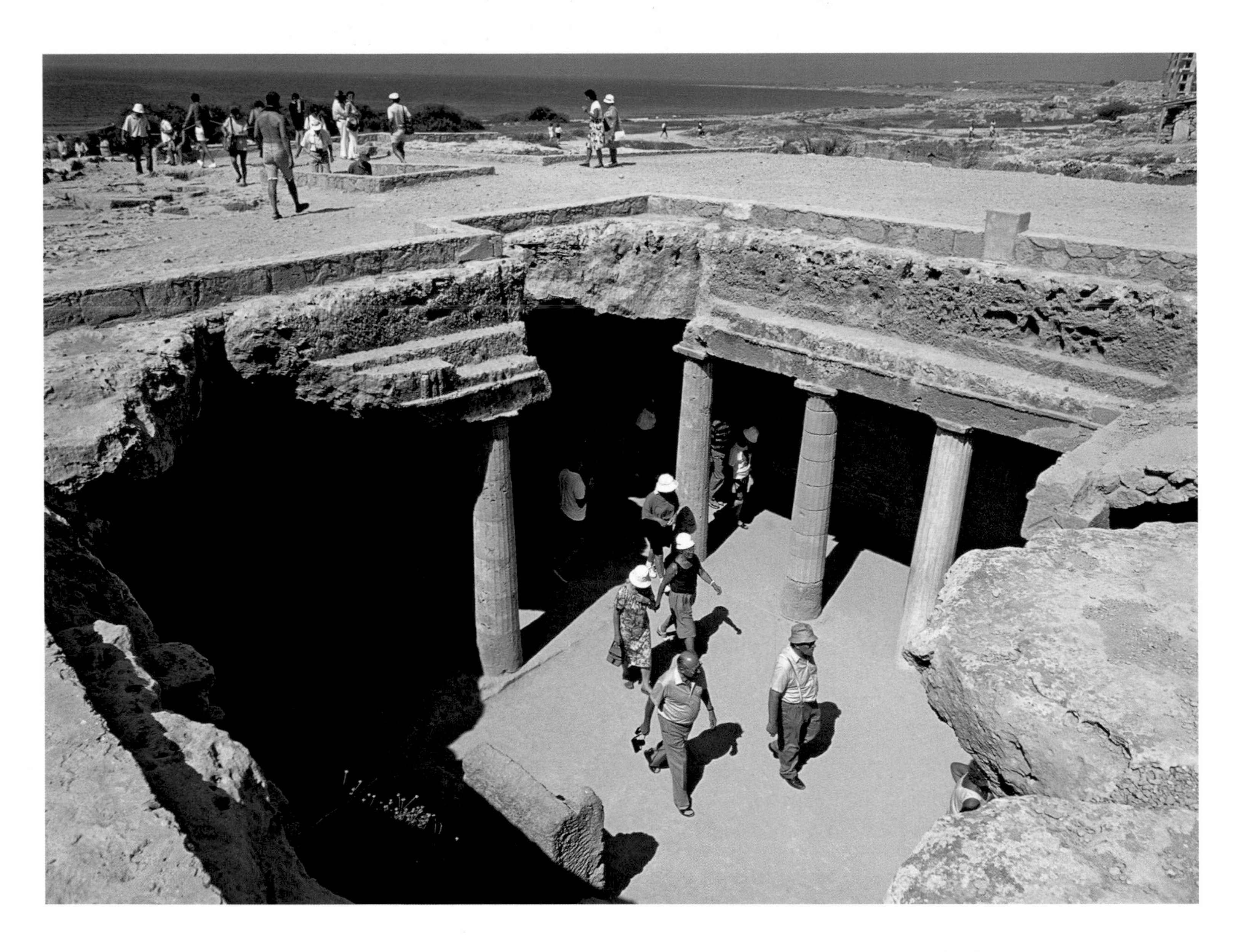

Above and opposite: Sightseers exploring the Tombs of the Kings, a complex of rock-cut chambers, where leading citizens of Pafos were interred during the city's Hellenistic and Roman periods.

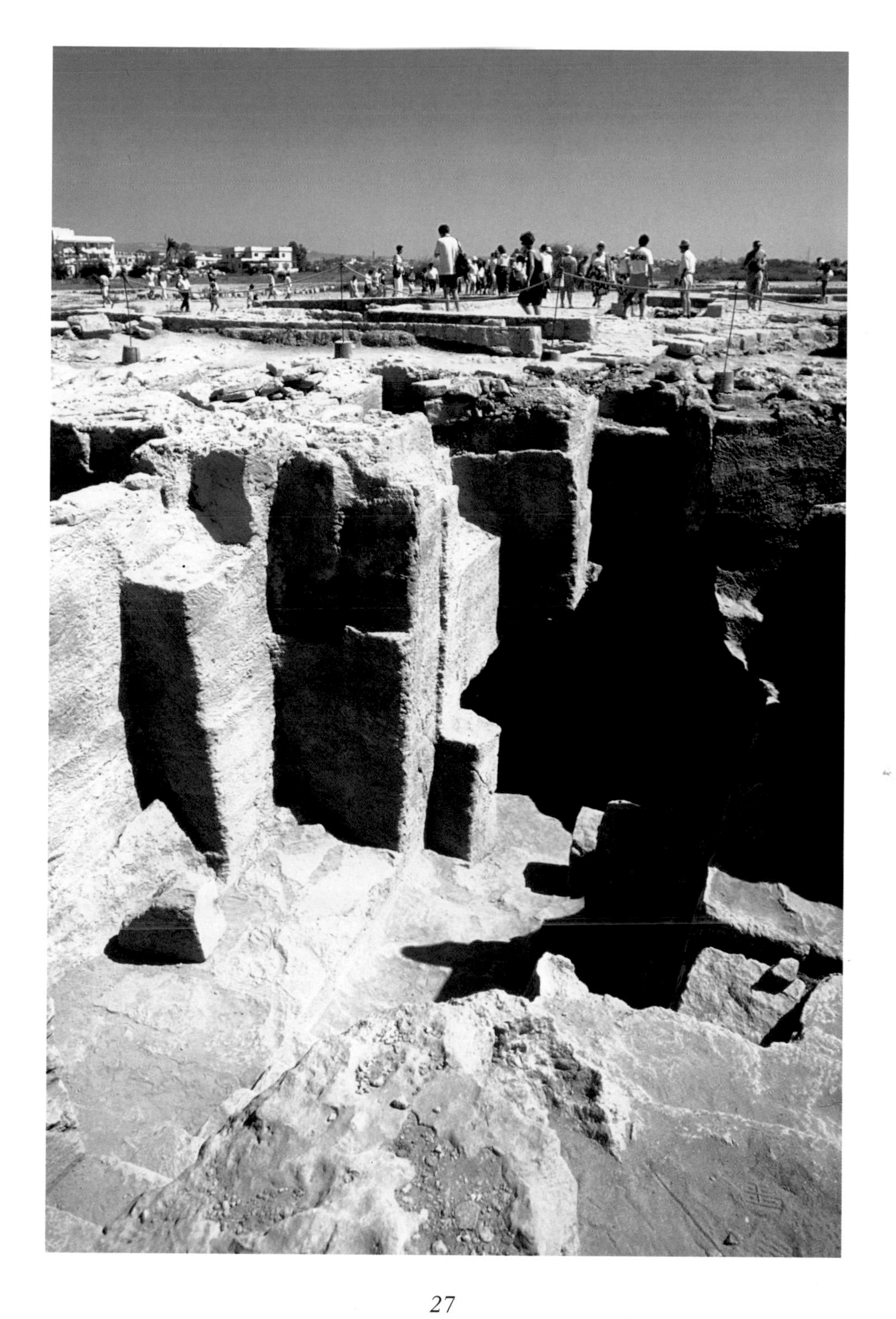

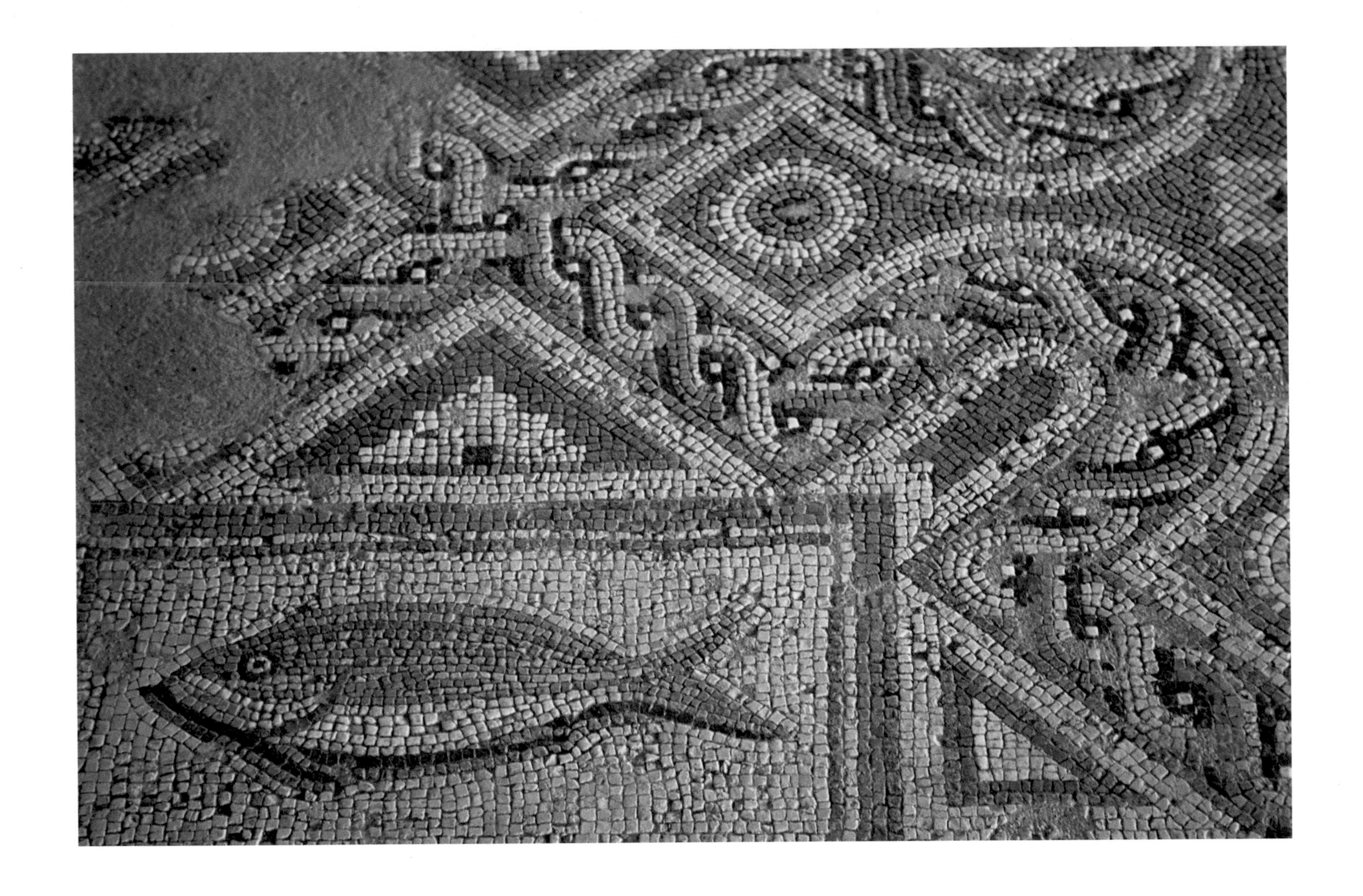

Detail of one of the mosaics of Pafos, depicting a fish. The mosaics were discovered in a cluster of buildings of the Roman period, principally the 3rd century AD.

Opposite: Petra tou Romiou, a rock formation that stands in shallow water off a beach in southwest Cyprus. The name literally means 'The Rock of the Great'.

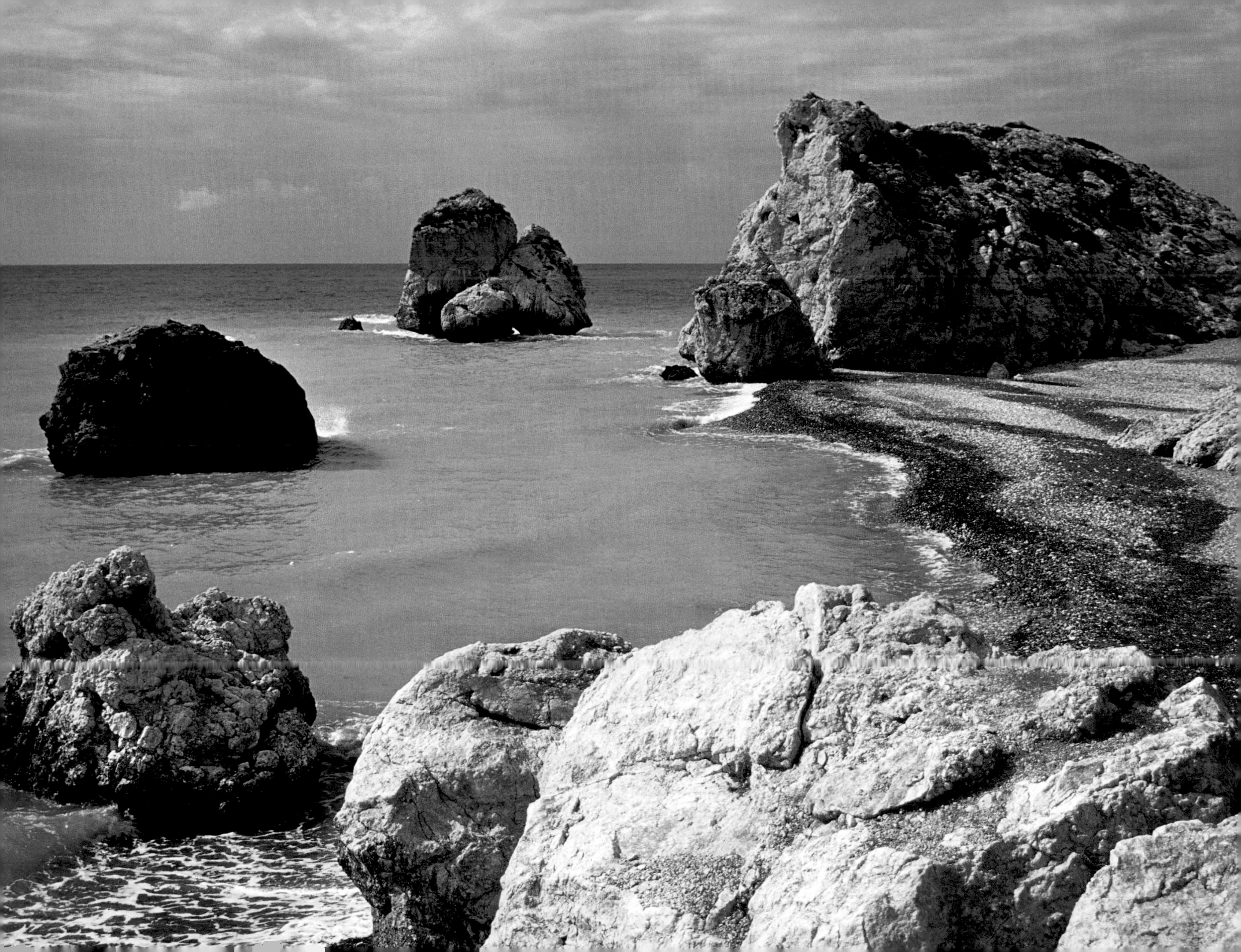

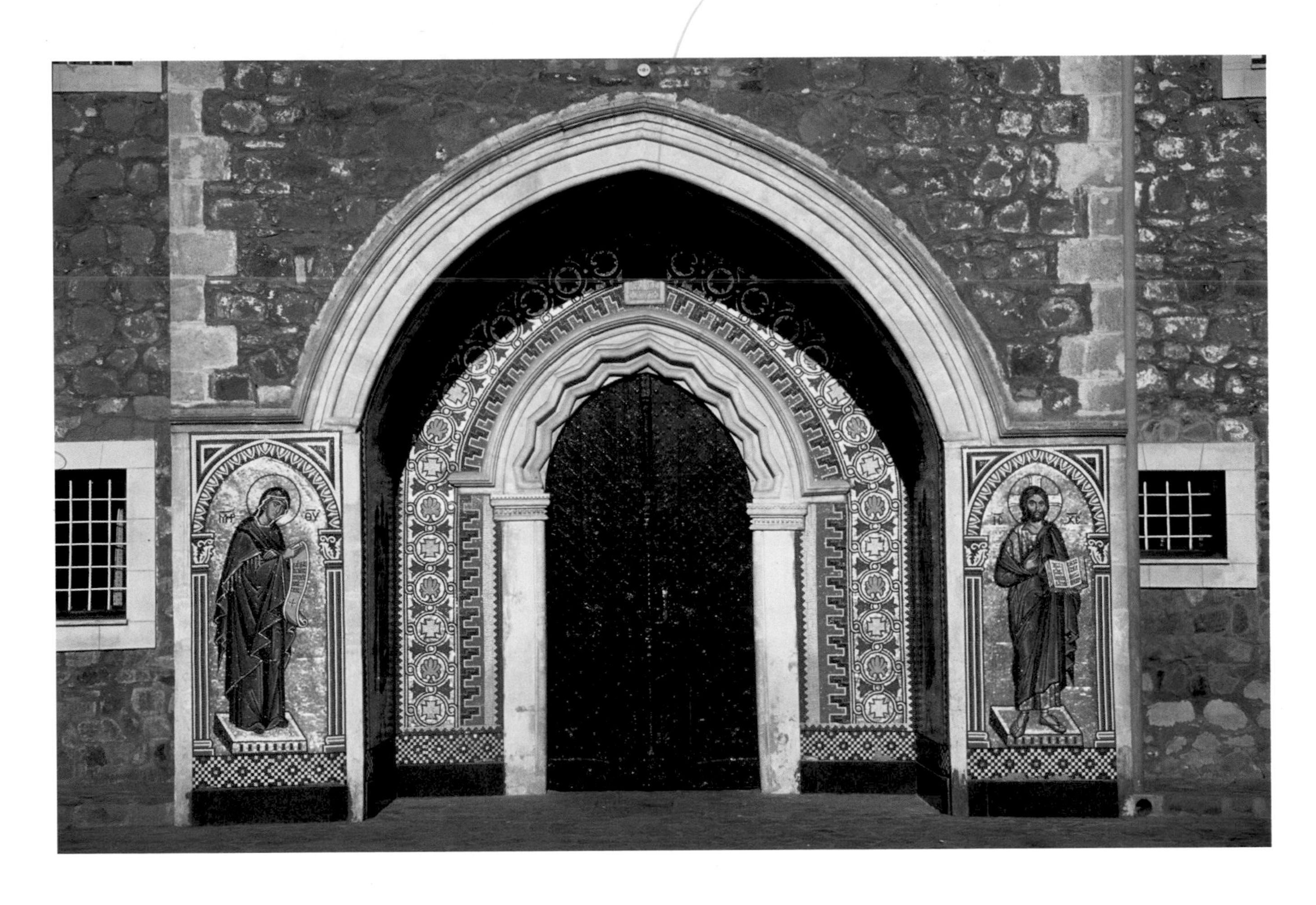

Two mosaics on either side of the entrance at Kykkos Monastery.

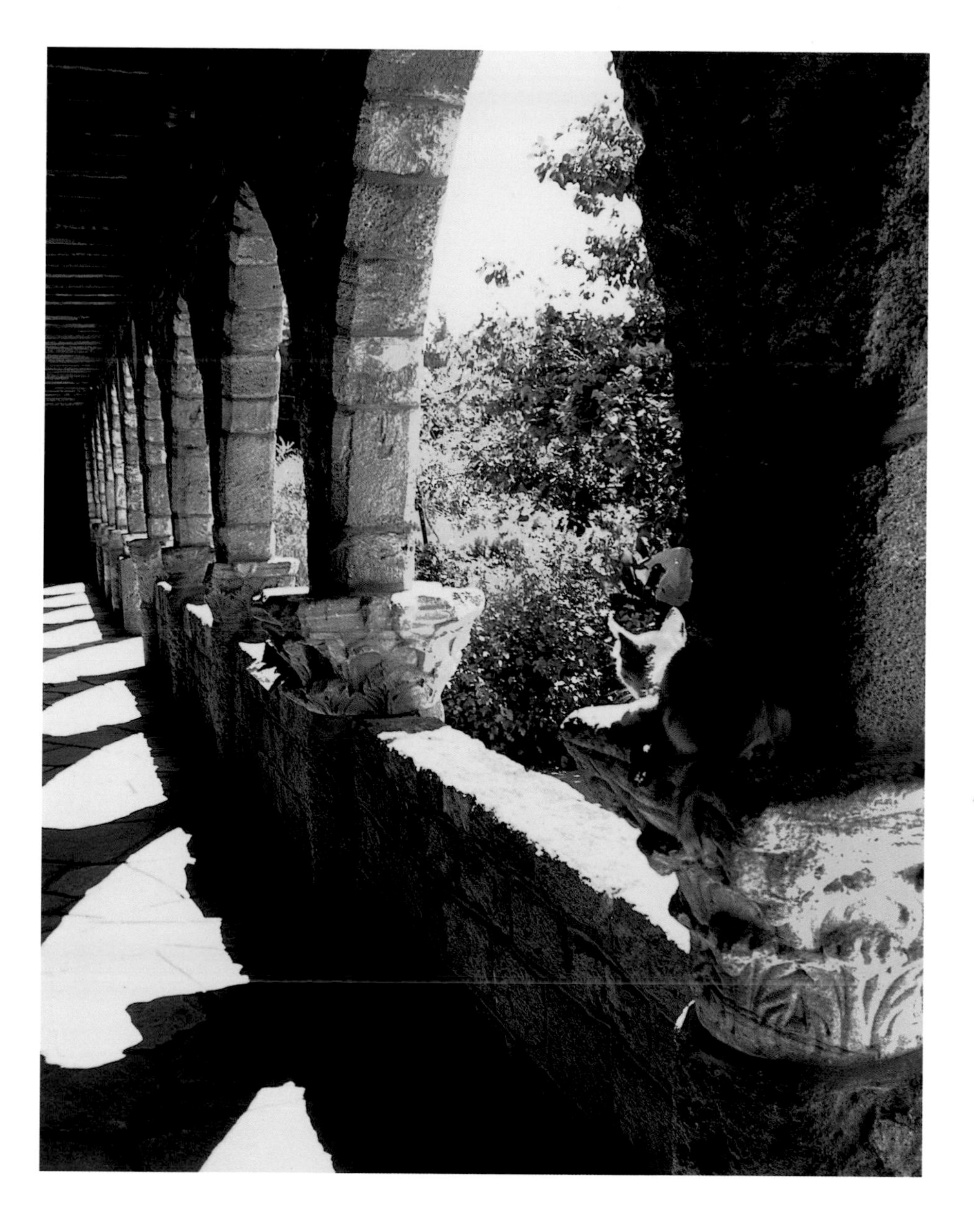

A resident perches on a column in the monastery of Agios Nikolaos ton Gaton (St Nicholas of the Cats), founded during the reign of Constantine (AD 324–37) and restored in the 13th century.

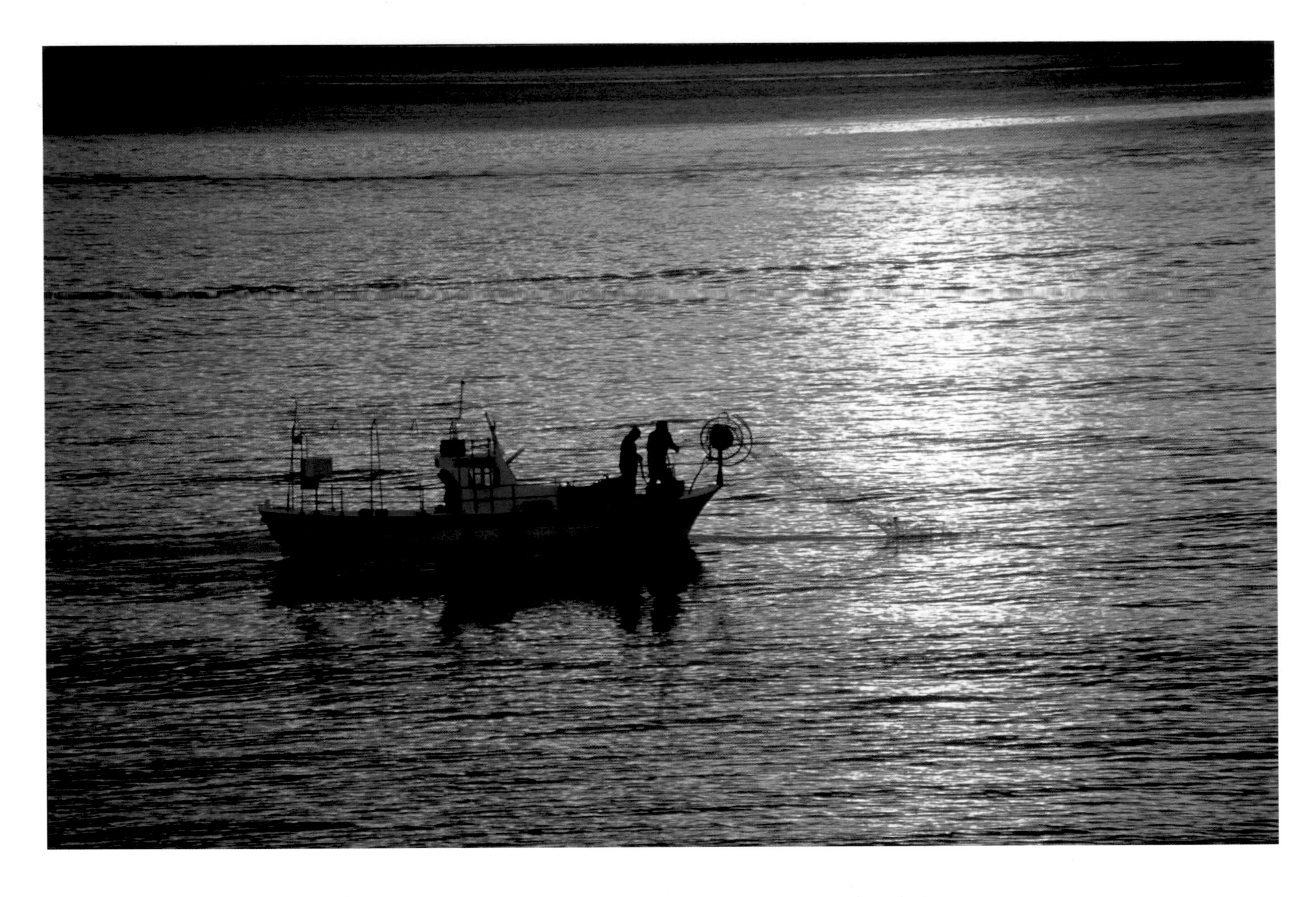

A fishing boat reeling in the last catch of the day in Larnaka's harbour.

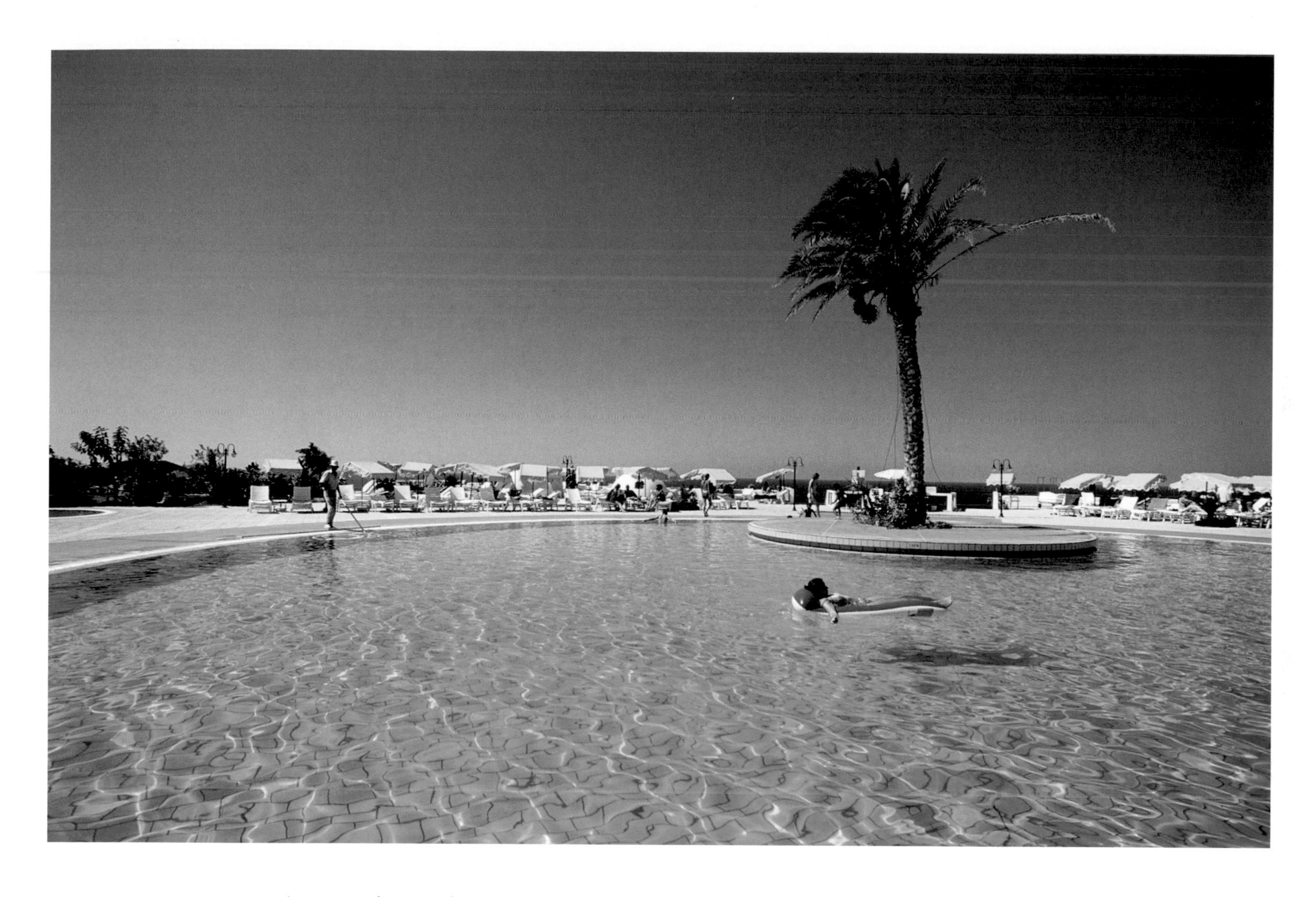

A sun-worshipper relaxes in the azure water of the large swimming pool of the Pafos Hotel.

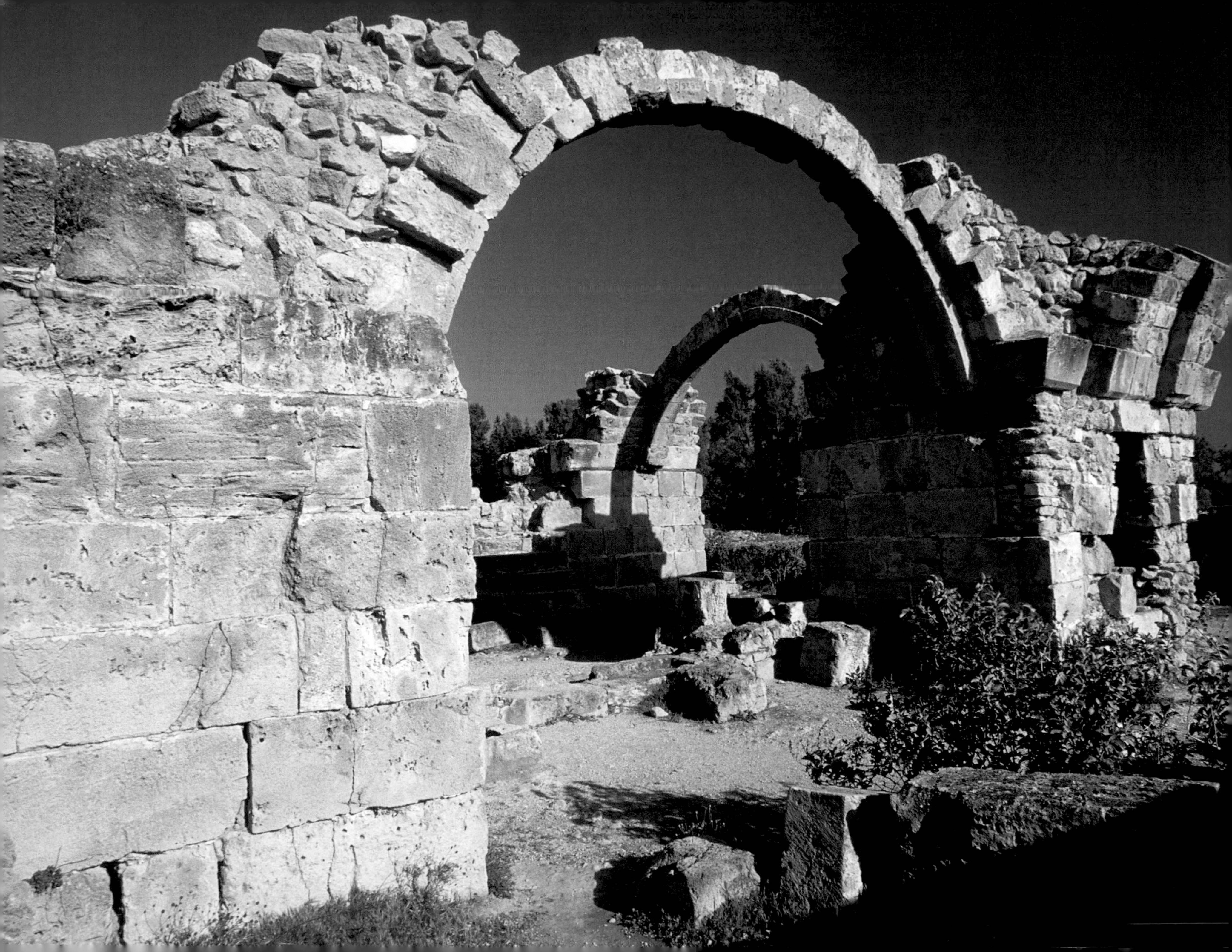

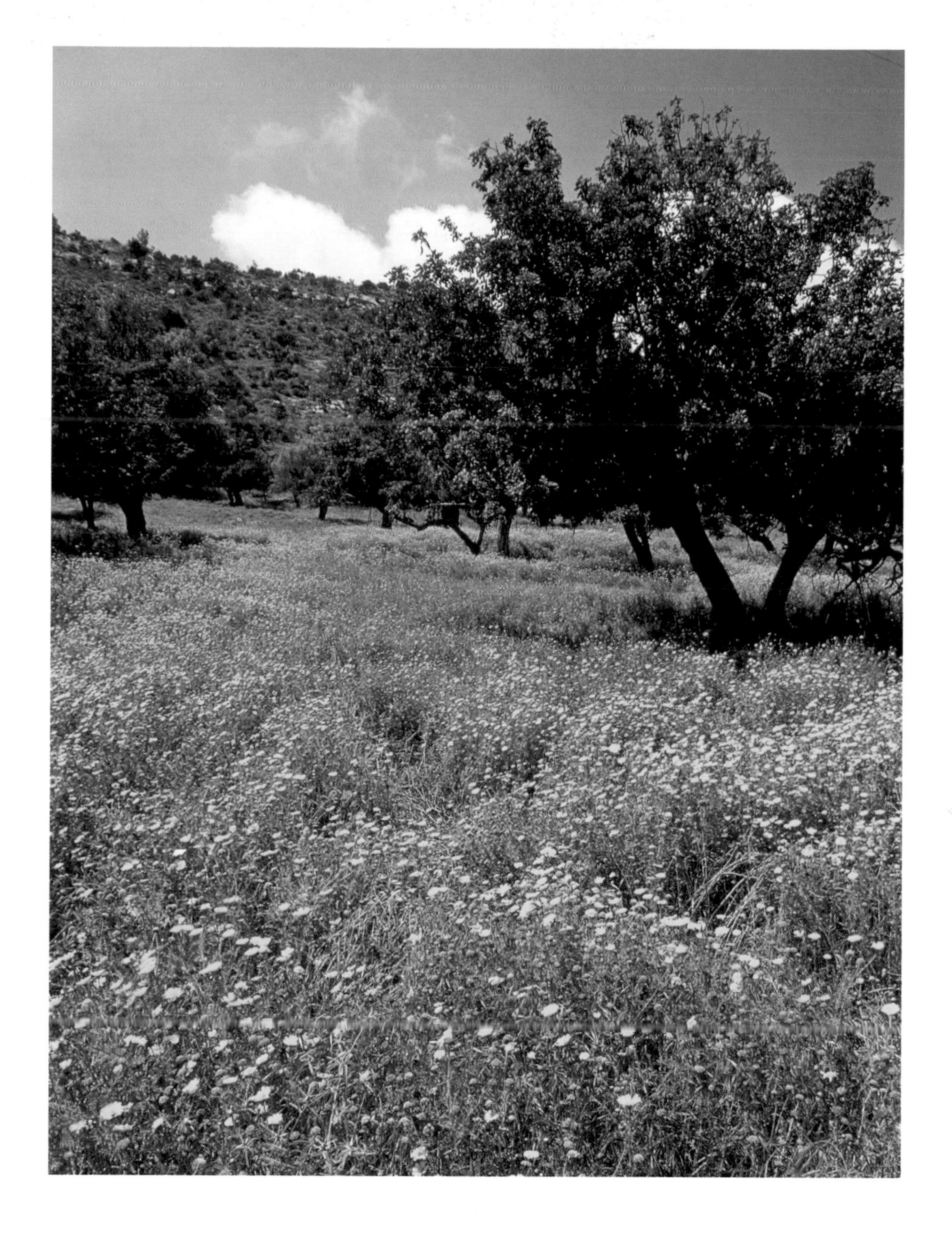

Yellow wildflowers cover a field in the Akamas Peninsula.
Opposite: The ruins of the medieval fort at Saranta Kolones, which was destroyed by an earthquake in the 13th century.

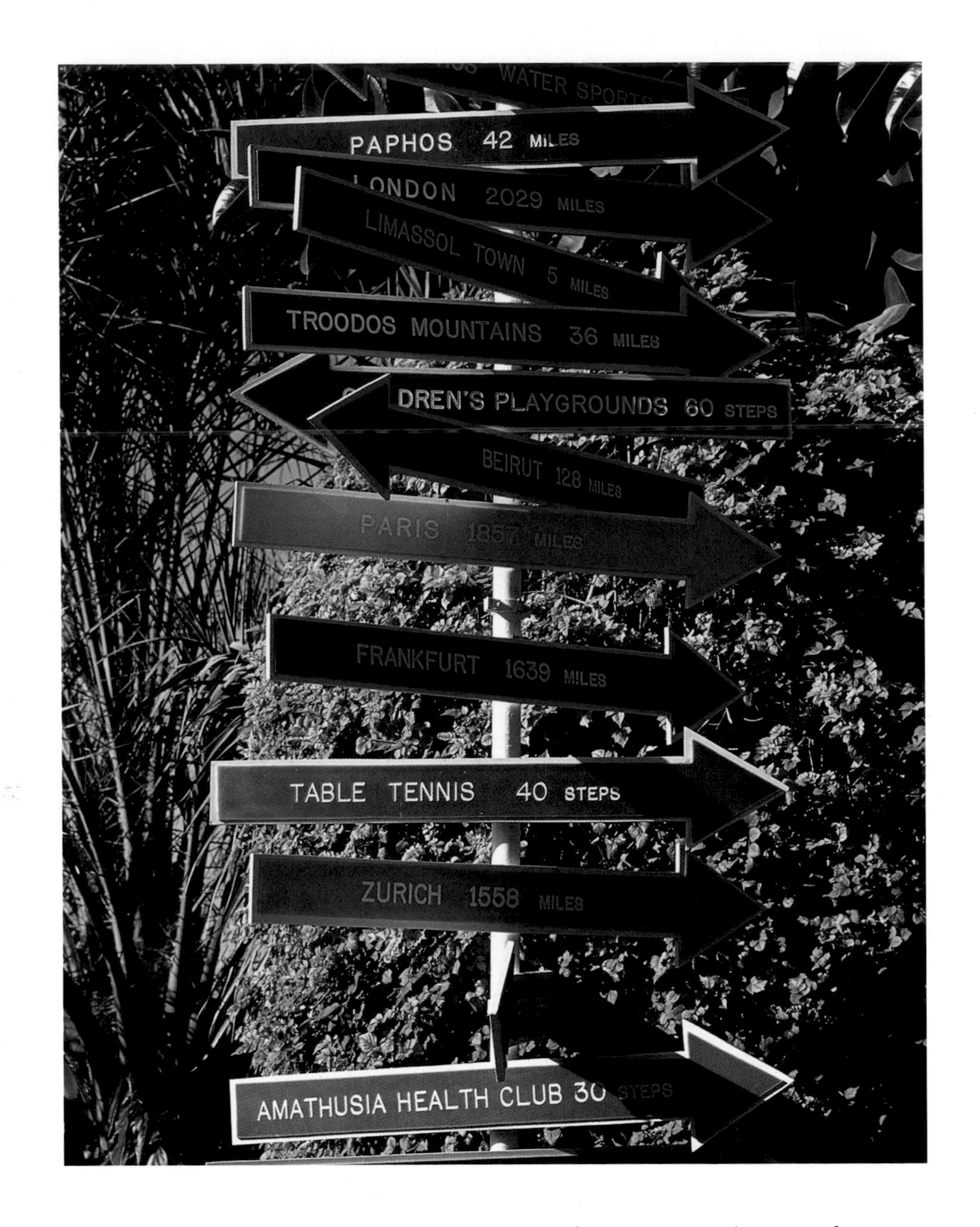

A host of signs point to some of the attractions of Cyprus — and to some famous places a bit further afield.

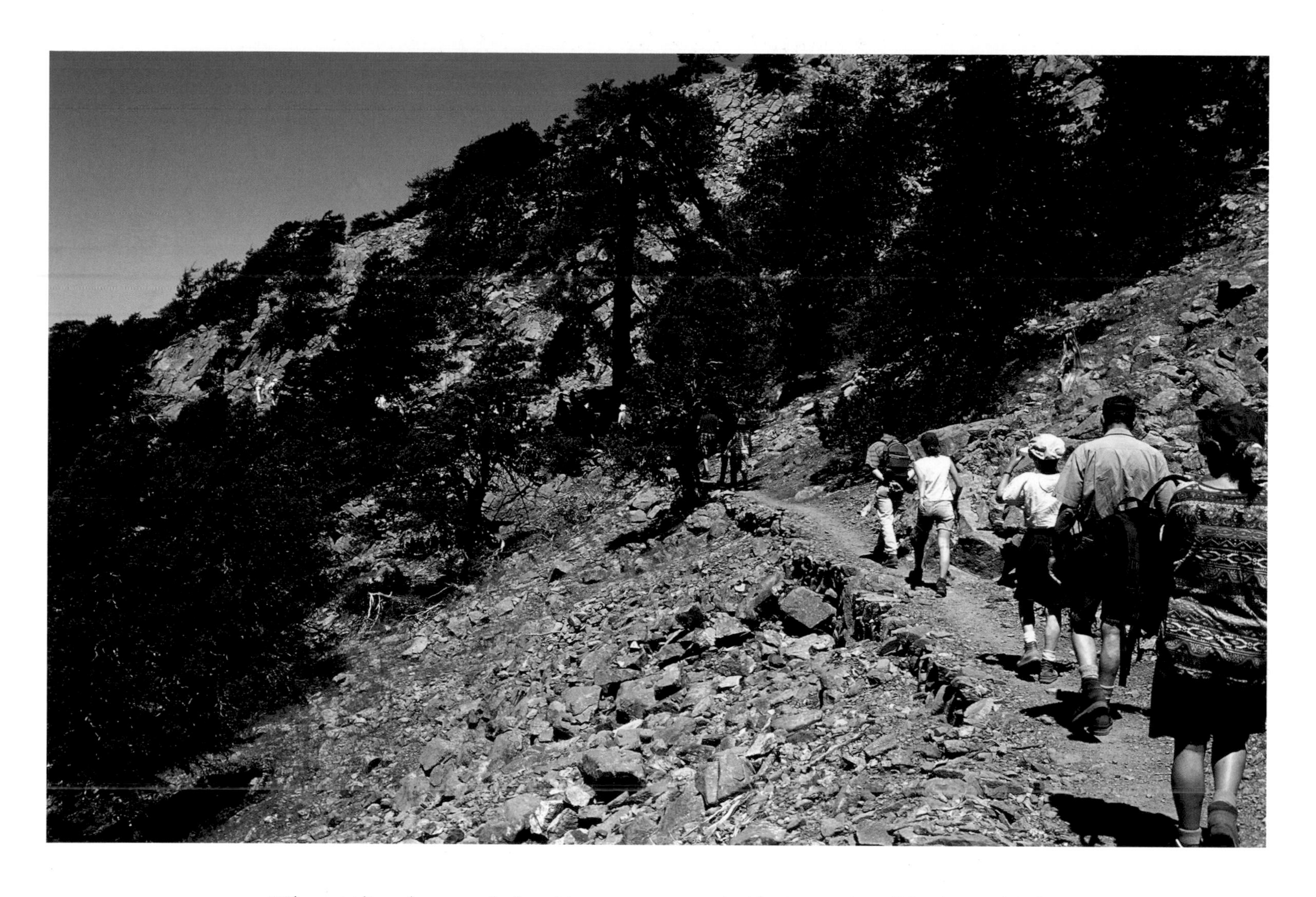

Hikers striding along a path that skirts a steep mountainside on a section of the Artemis Trail. The trail is a 4-mile (7-km) circular walk around the upper slopes of Mount Olympos.

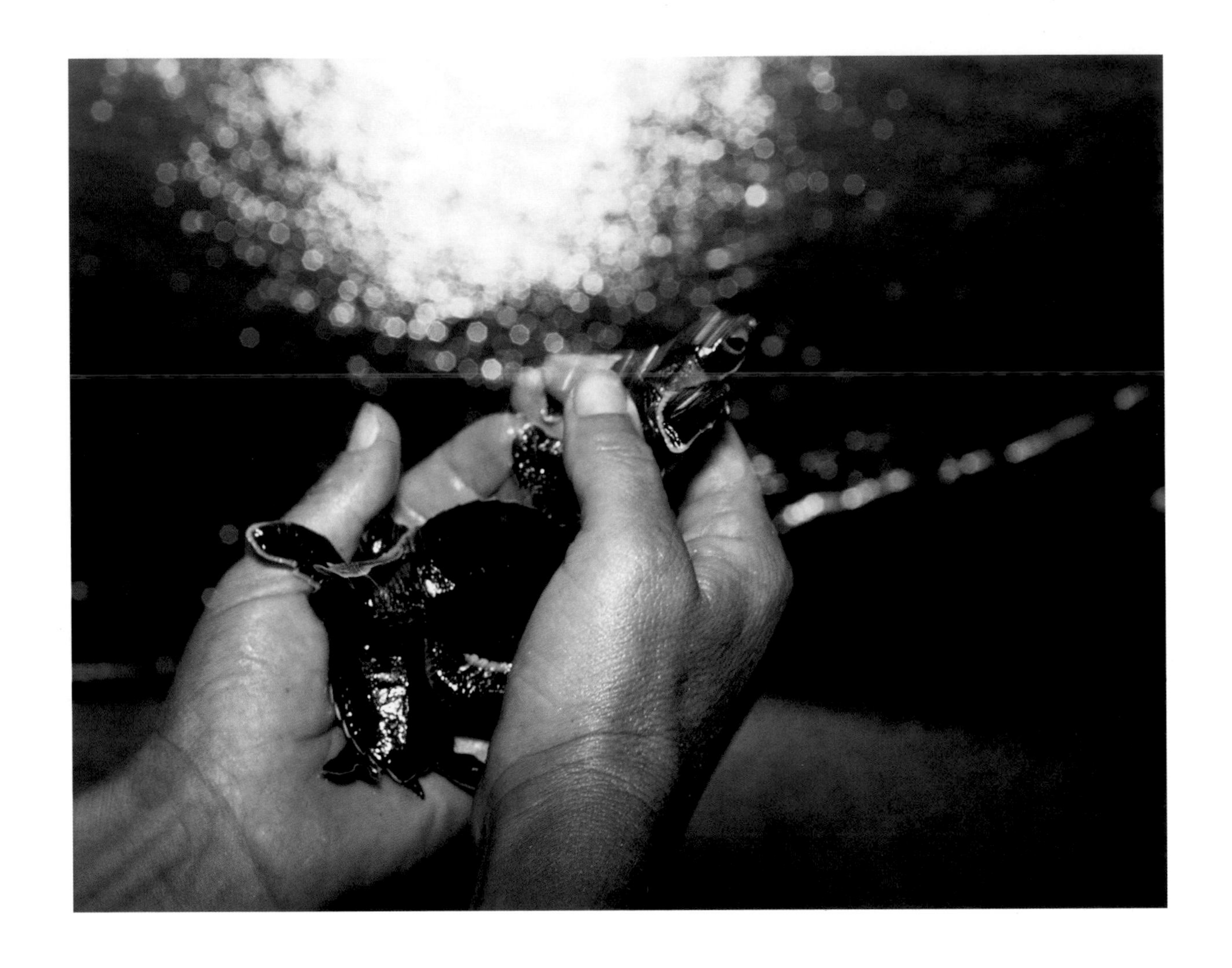

A member of the Lara Project cradles some newly born loggerhead turtles.
The aim of the project is to protect the turtles' birthplace.
Opposite: Waves lap onto the sands of Lara Bay, where the turtles lay their eggs
under the protection of the Lara Project

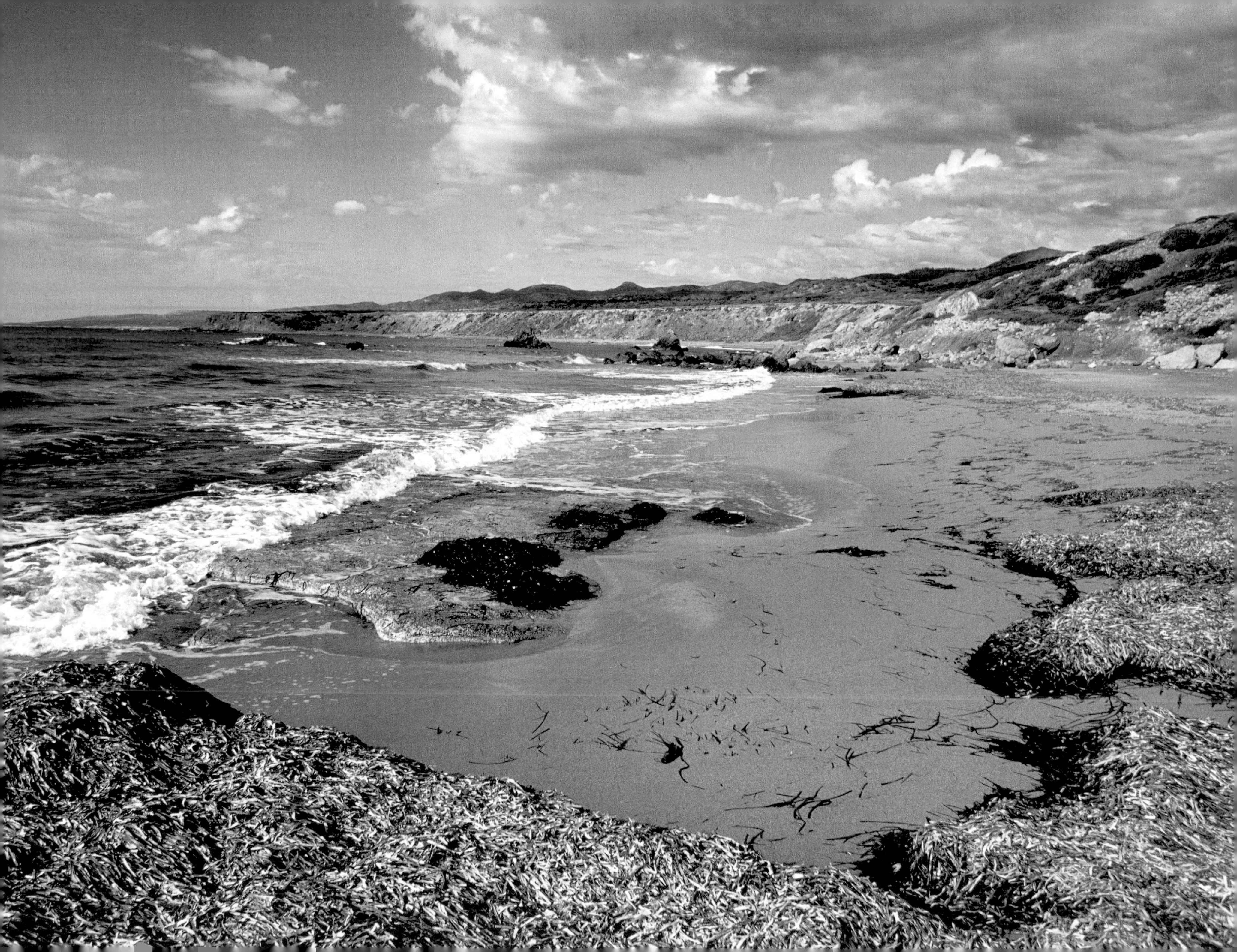

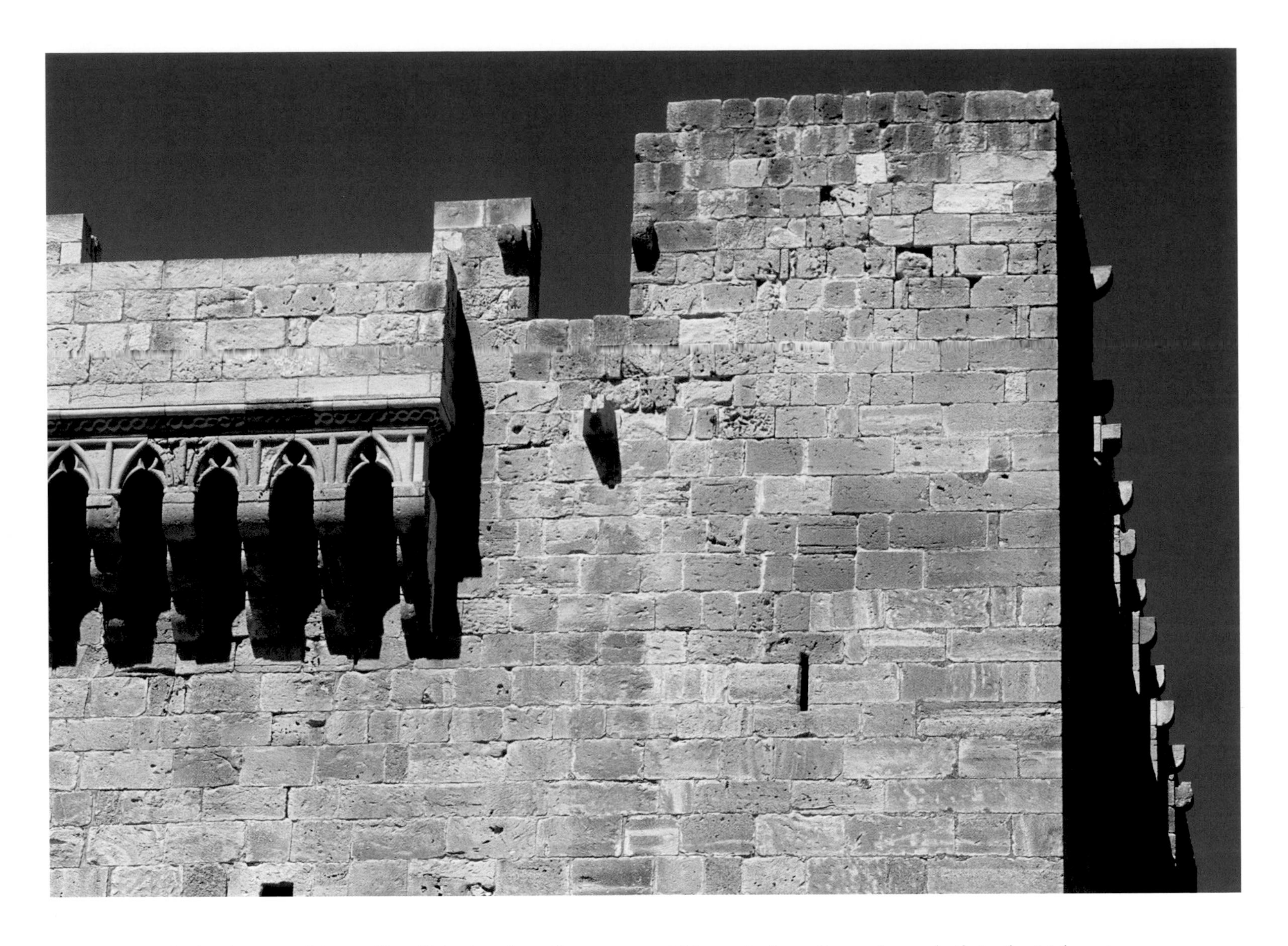

The battlements of the castle at Kolossi, a short distance west of Limassol. An earlier castle was built in the 13th century for the Knights of St John. The present one was built by the Knights in the 15th century.

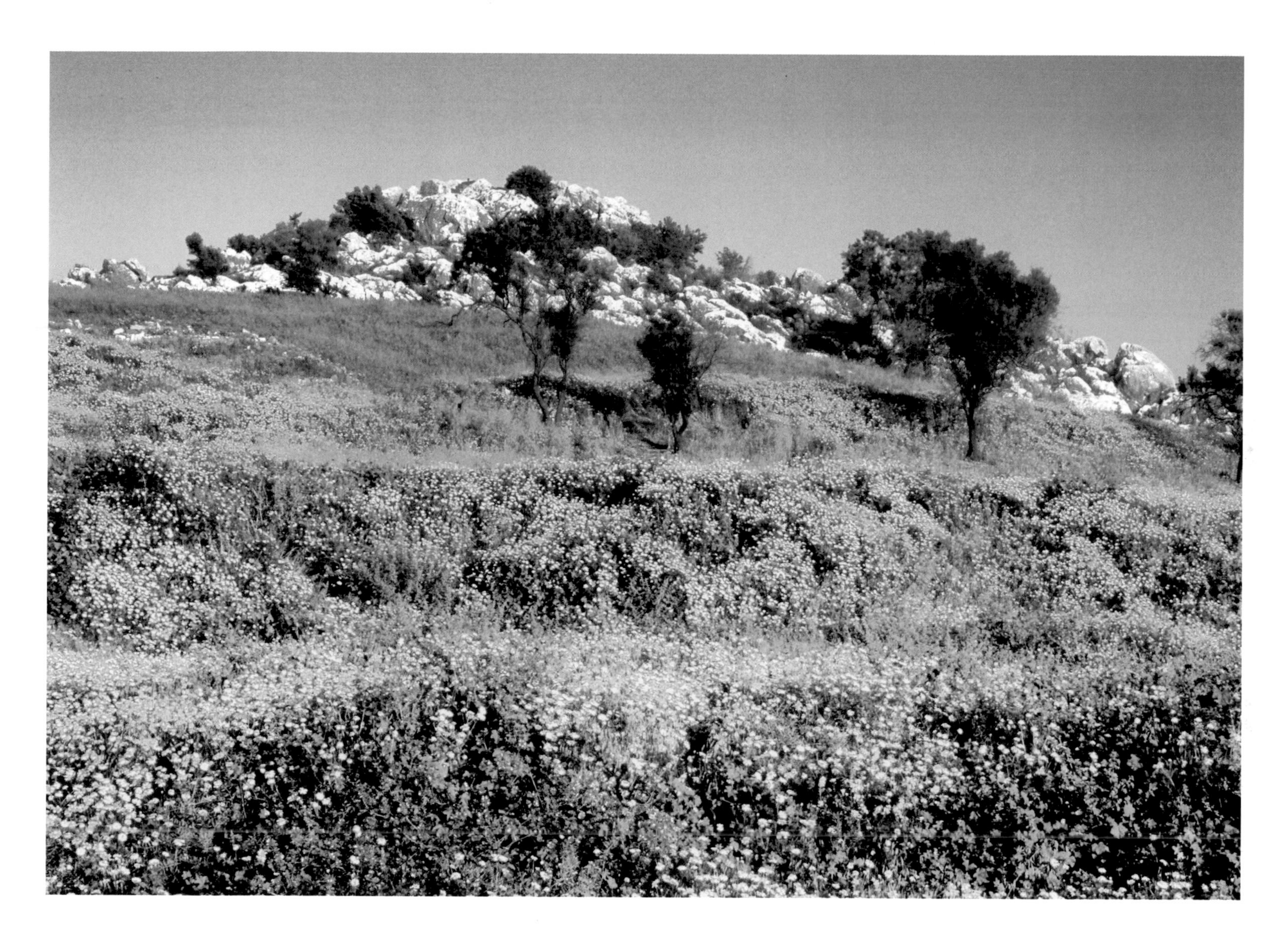

Marigolds lend a golden hue to the floor of the Xeros Potamos Valley.

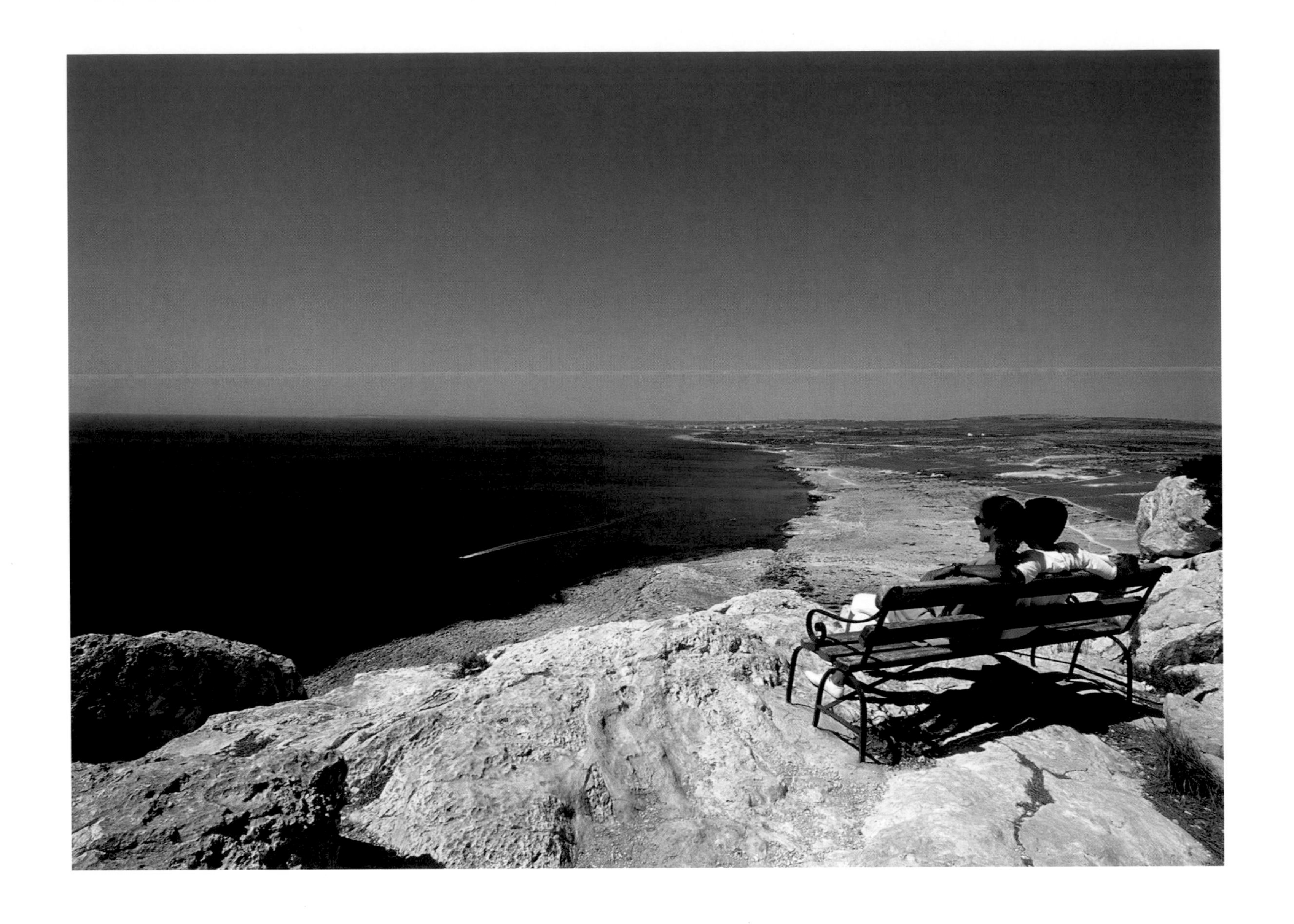

The blue waters of the Mediterranean surround the low headland of Cape Gkreko on the southeastern corner of Cyprus.

Aphrodite's Rock (also known as Petra tou Romiou) at sunset.

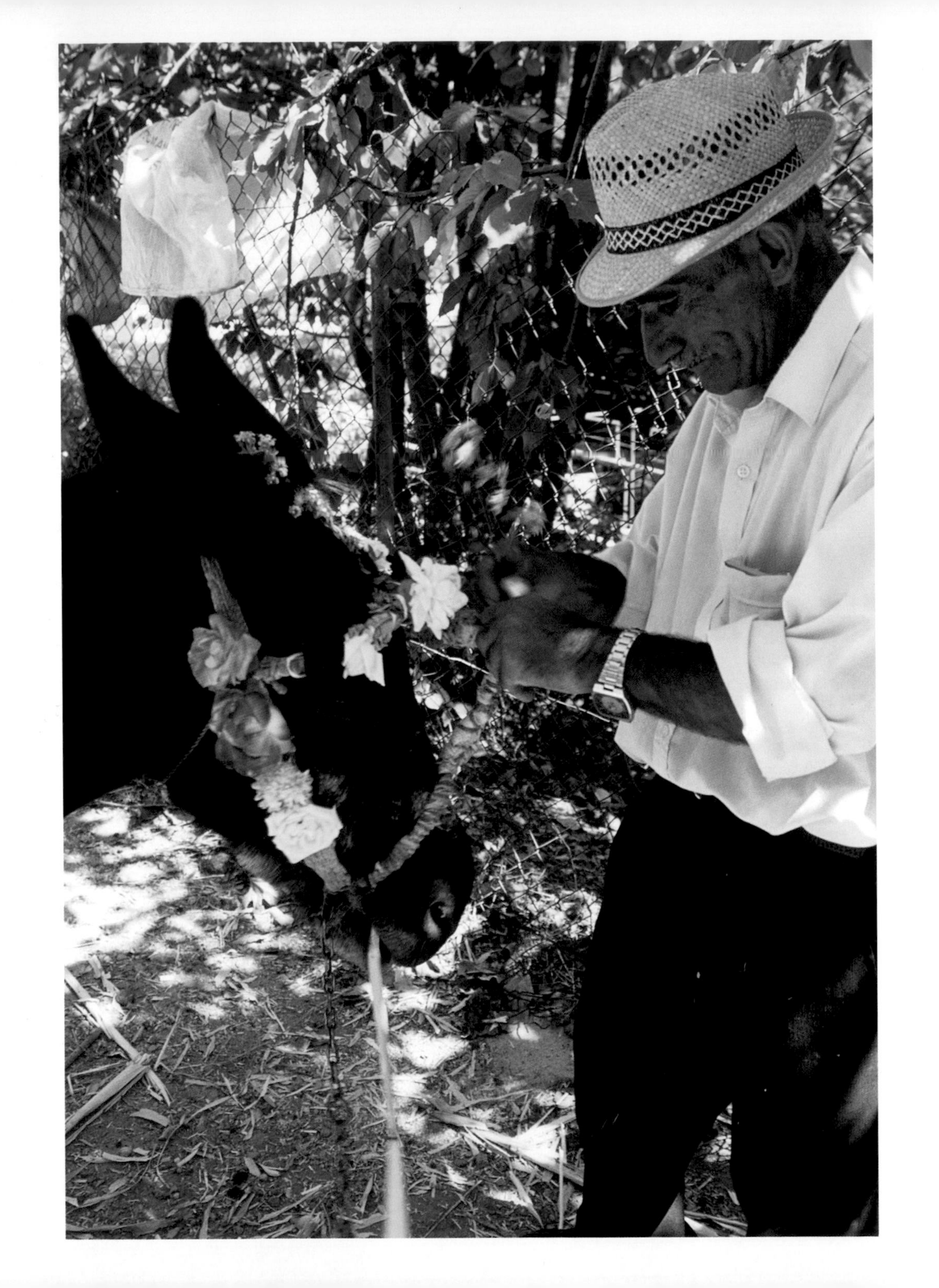

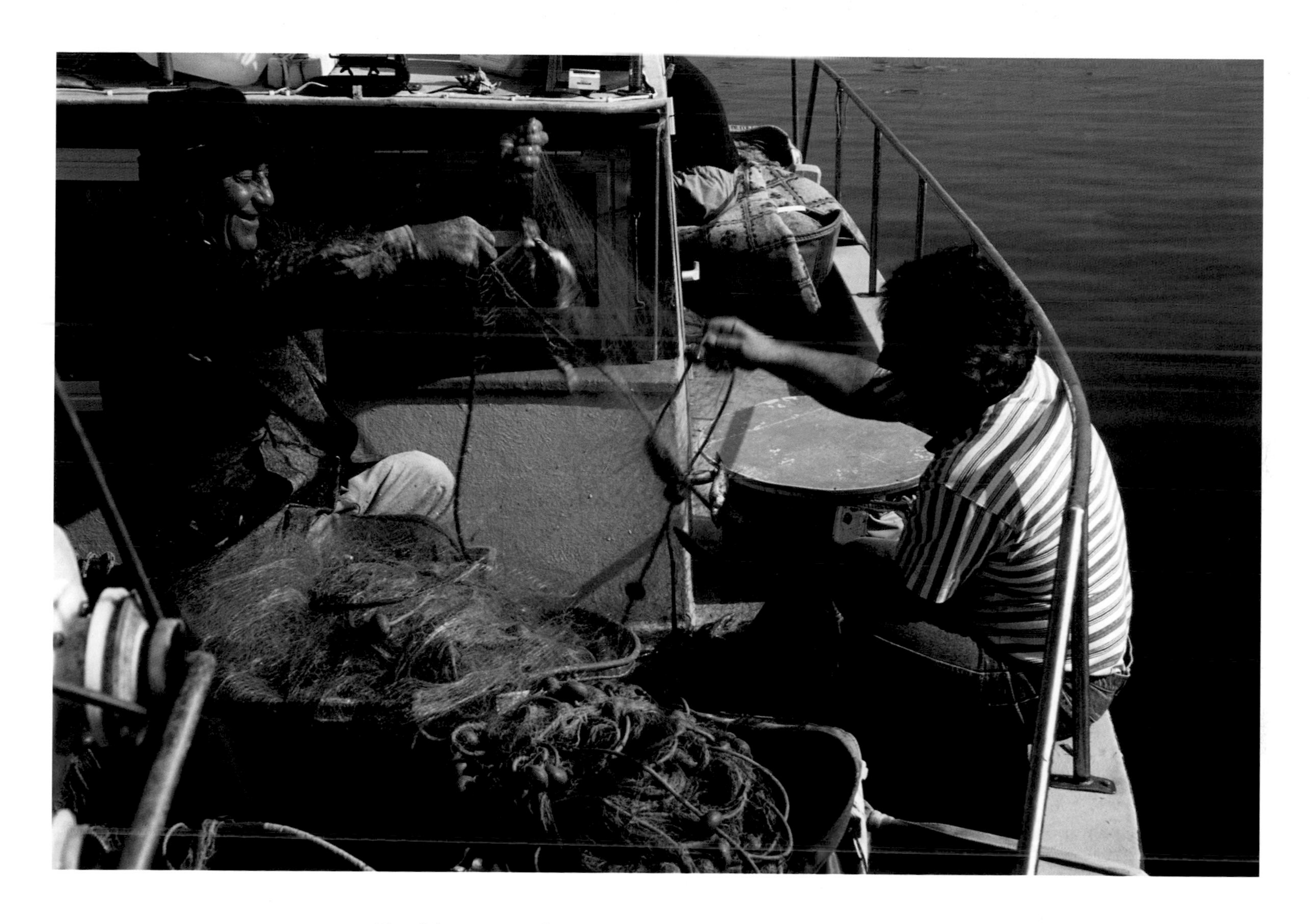

Two fishermen sort their catch on a fishing boat in Larnaka harbour.
Opposite: A traditional Cypriot donkey is given some finishing touches in readiness for a wedding.

The Salt Lake is situated just outside Larnaka. Adjacent to it lies the Hala Sultan Tekkesi dedicated to the Prophet Mohammed's wet-nurse who died here. It is one of Islam's holiest shrines.

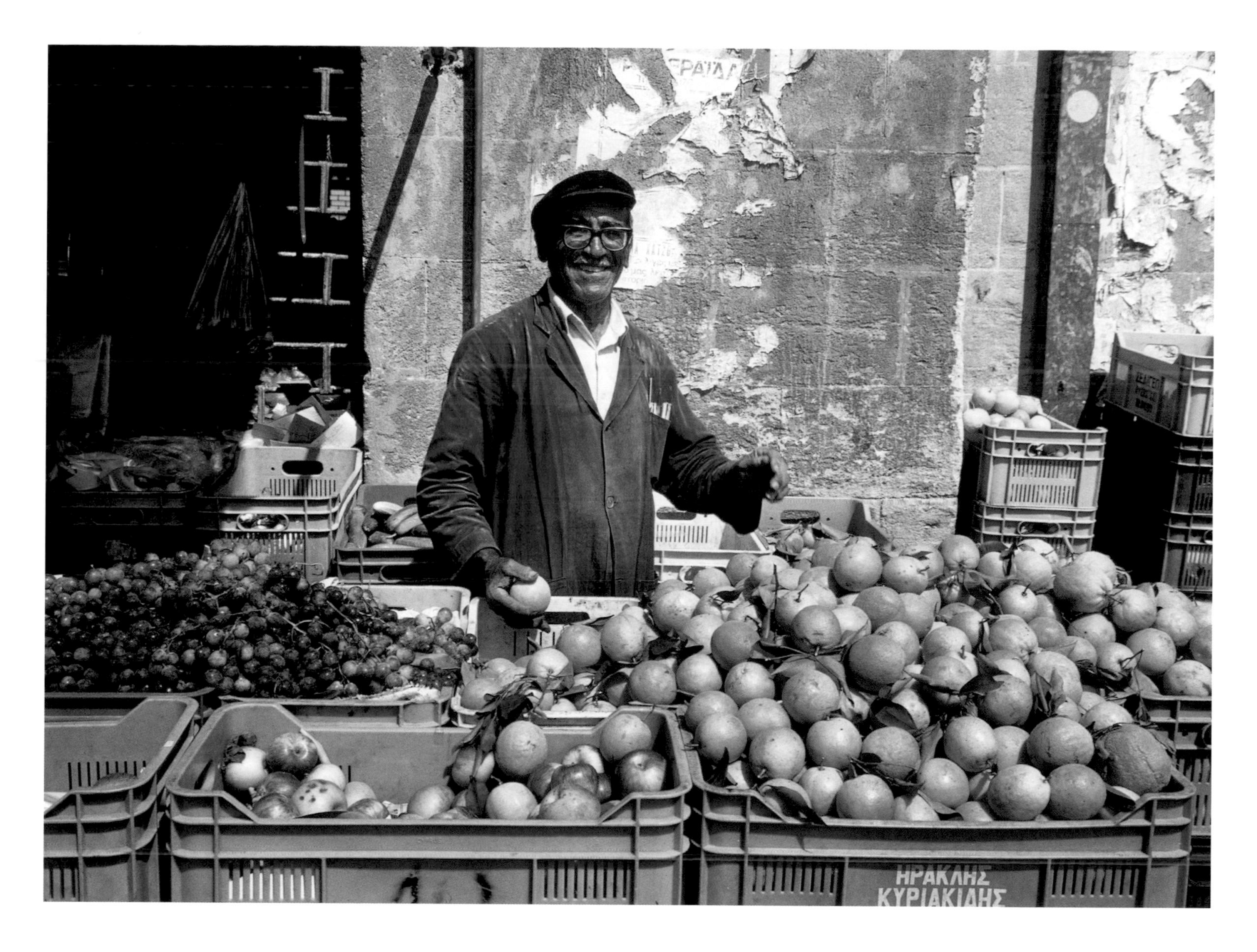

Fresh, locally grown fruit is piled high on a stall at the Municipal Market in Nicosia. Such markets are a feature of every village and town in Cyprus.

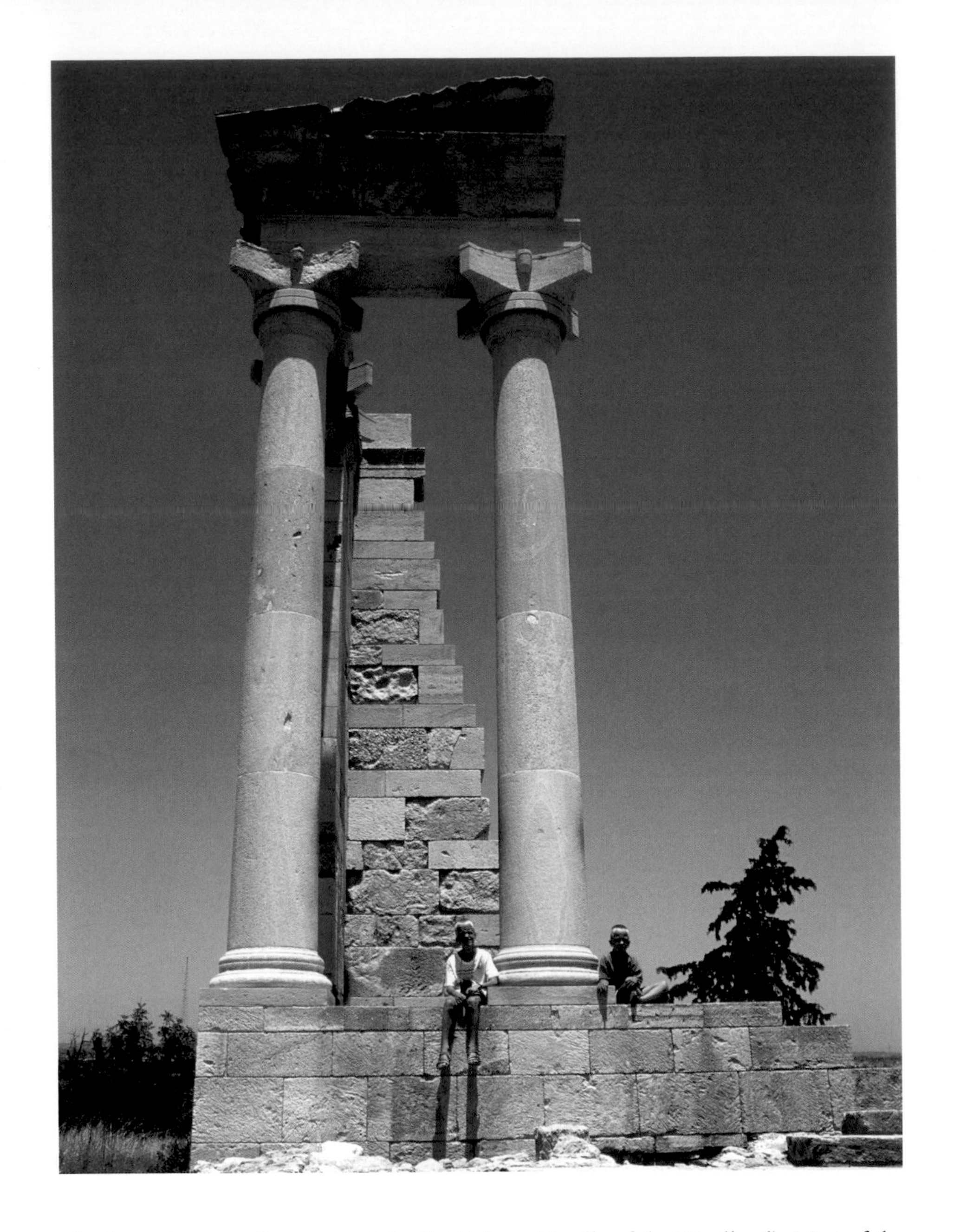

A colonnade at the Sanctuary of Apollo Hylates (Apollo of the Woodland). Most of the remains of the sanctuary date from a Roman restoration after an earthquake in AD 77.

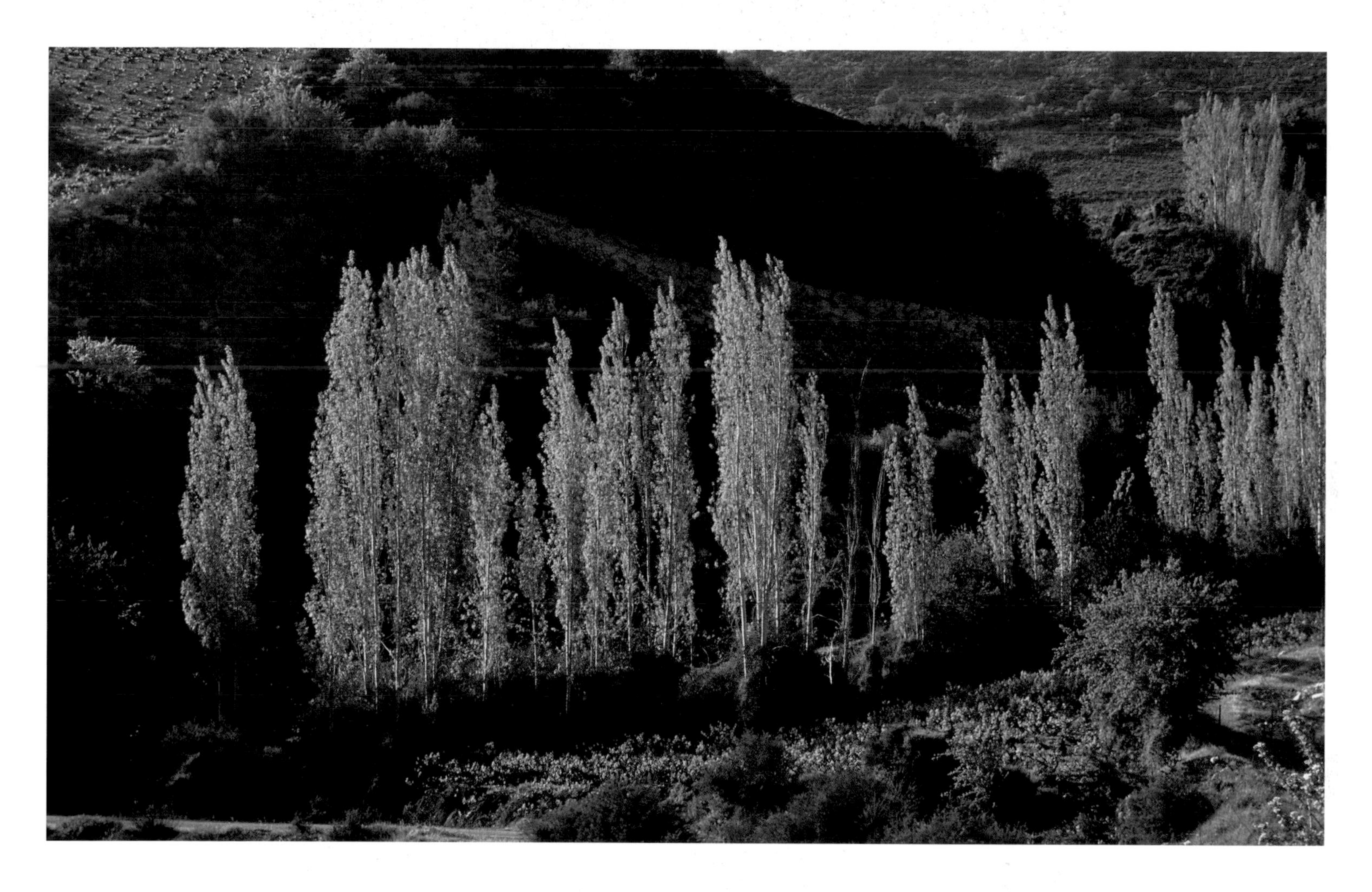

Forest landscape near Mandria, in the Troodos foothills.

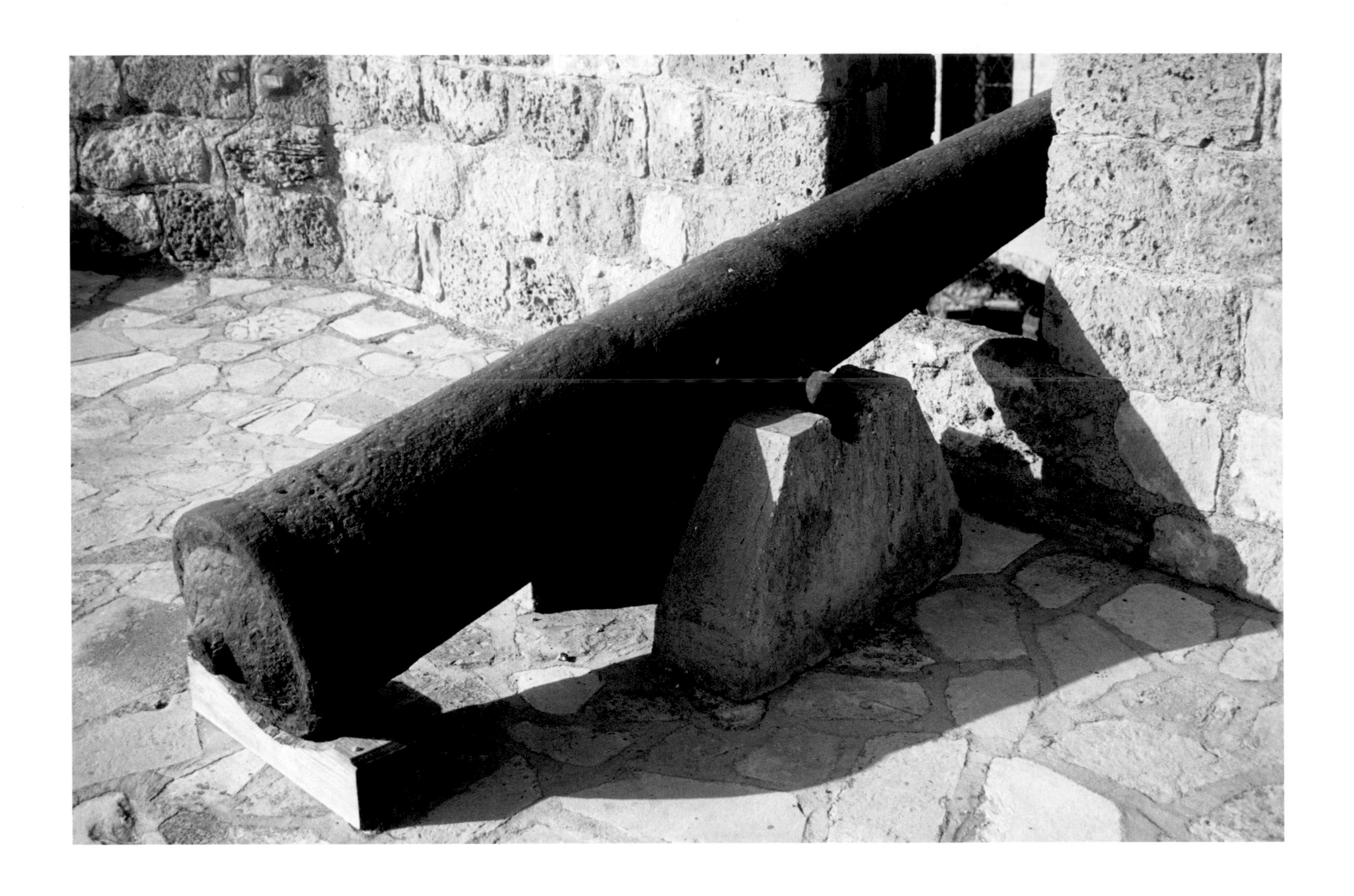

A corroded iron cannon on the battlements of the only original seaward-facing wall that survives today at the rectangular stone Larnaka Fort. The fort was built by the Ottoman governor in 1625.
Opposite: Tourists sitting on the steps of an ancient amphitheatre overlooking the Mediterranean and scrub-covered slopes. The amphitheatre is a feature of the ruined city of Kourion on the south coast of Cyprus.

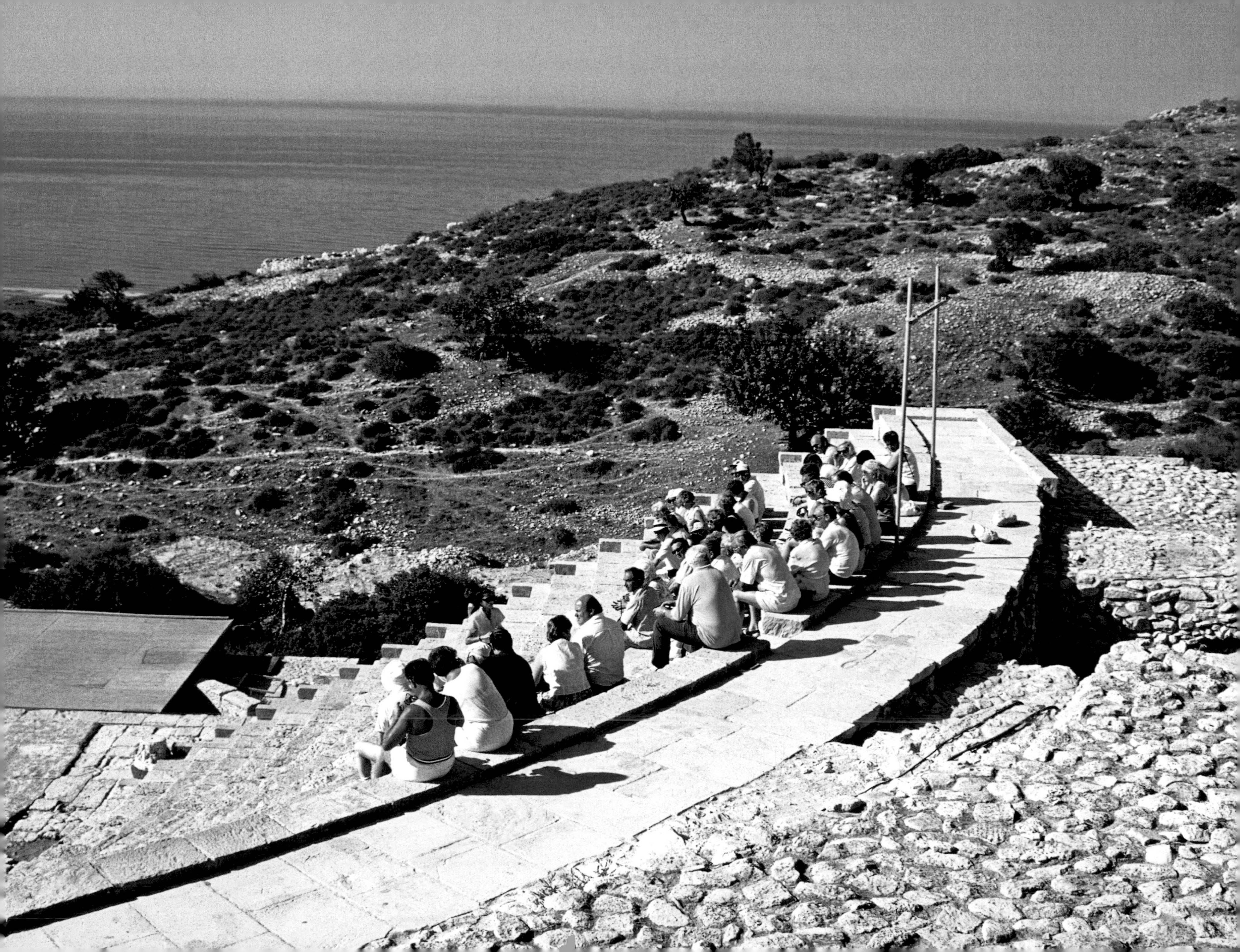

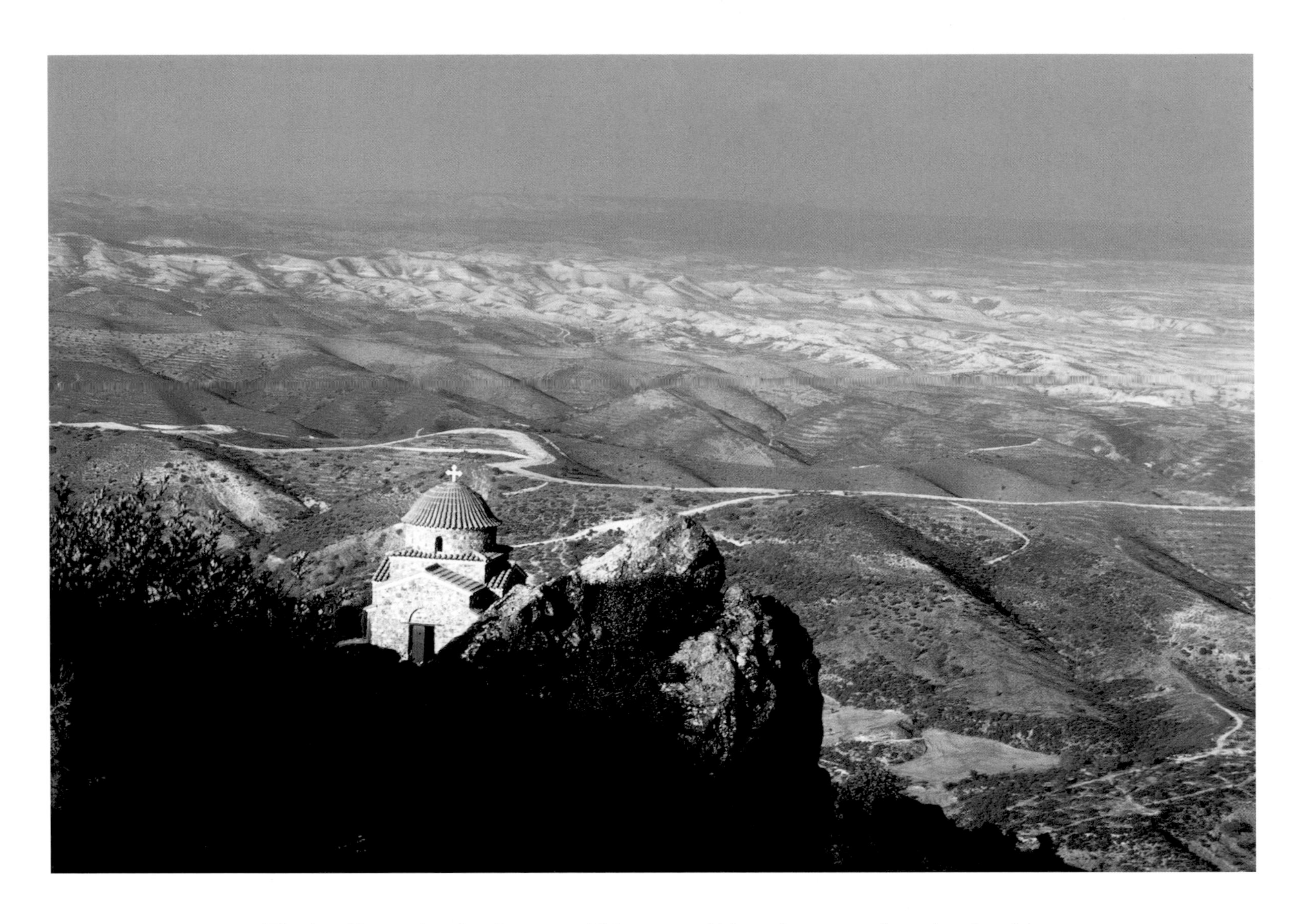

The Agia Varvara chapel at Stavrovouni Monastery, which perches on a peak on the edge of the Troodos Mountains, commands sweeping views of the surrounding countryside.

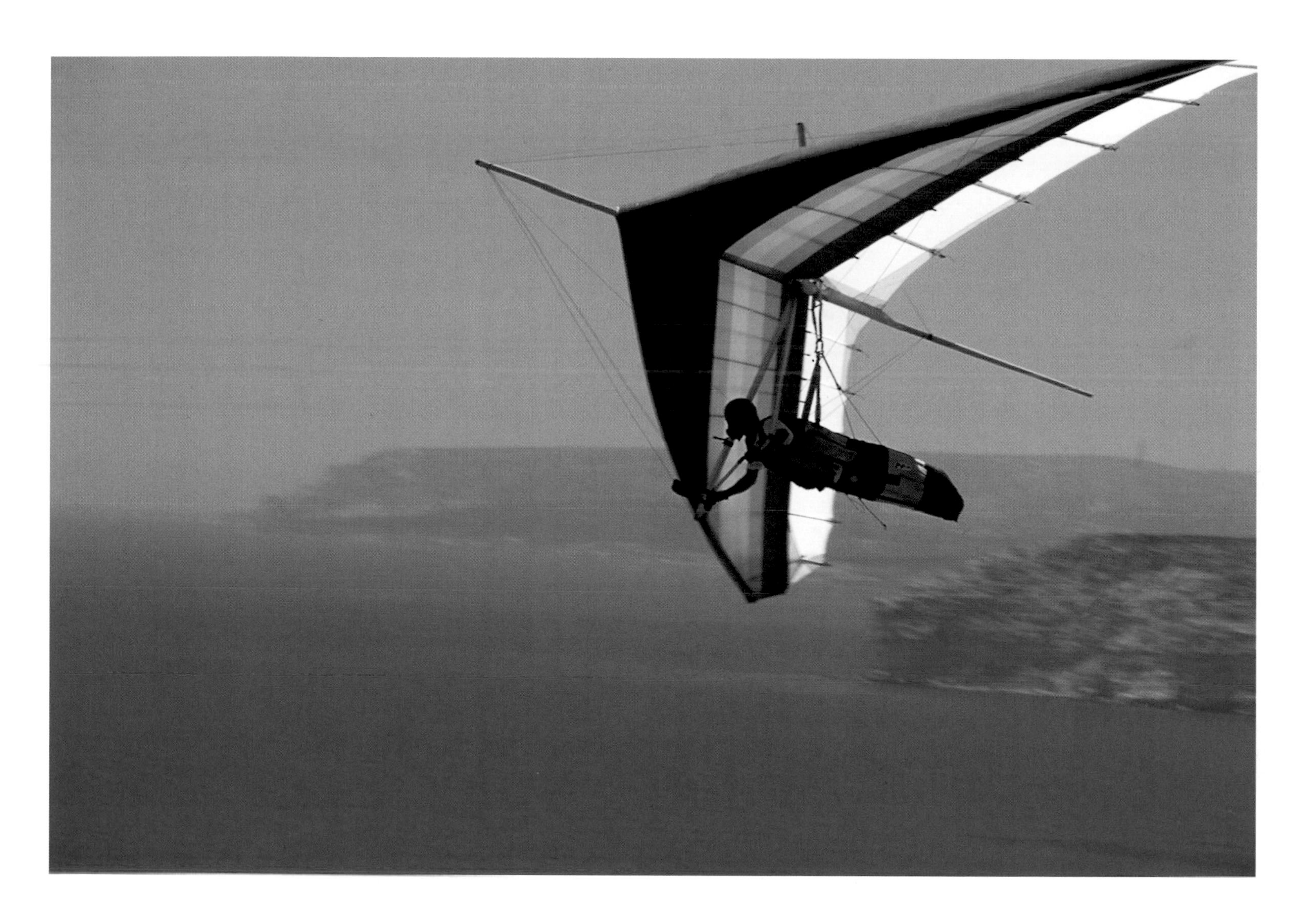

A hang-glider pilot riding thermals high above the ruins of the city of Kourion which overlooks the Mediterranean on the south coast of Cyprus.

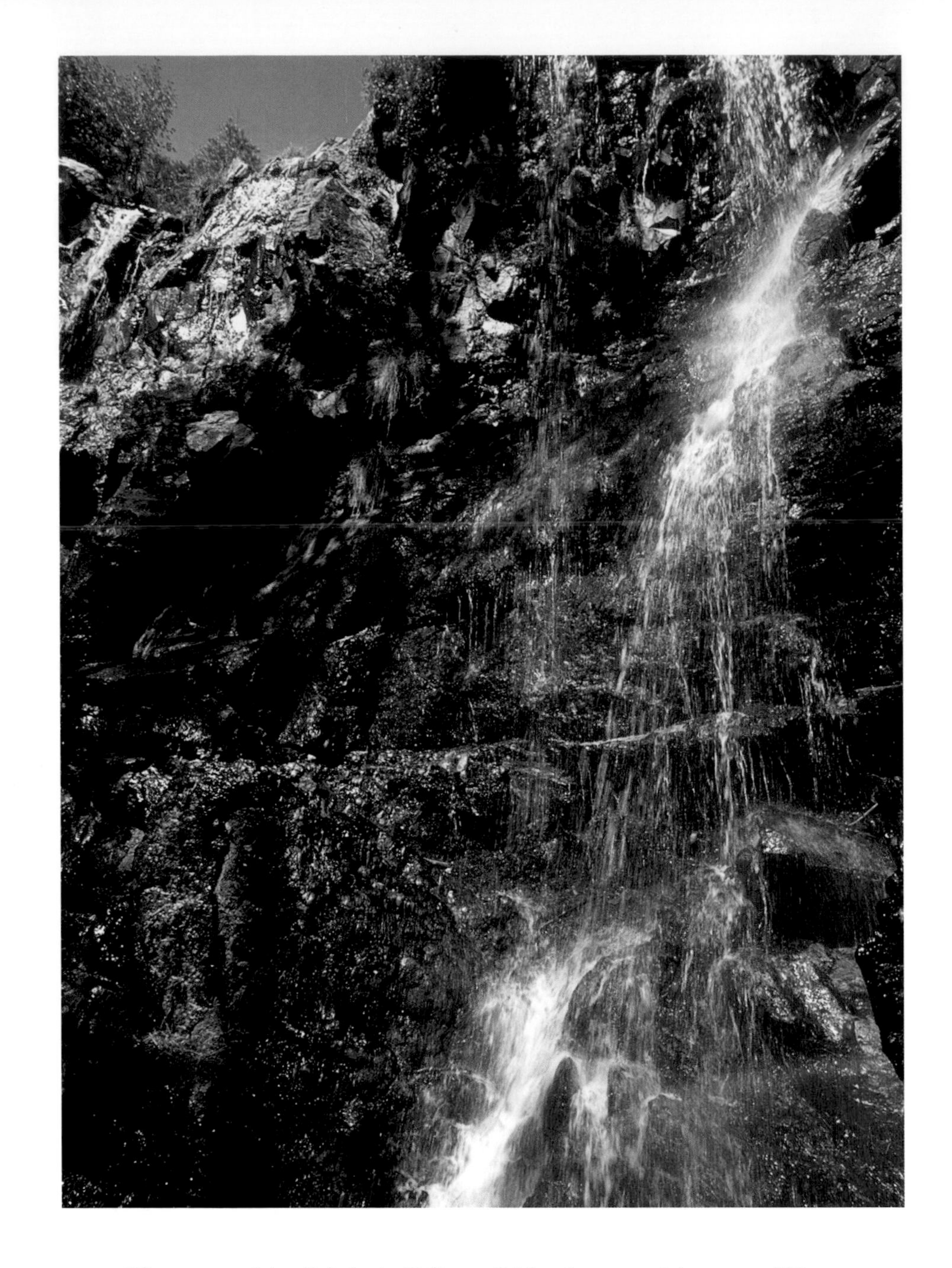

The waters of the Caledonia Falls are fed by the perennial stream of Kryos.

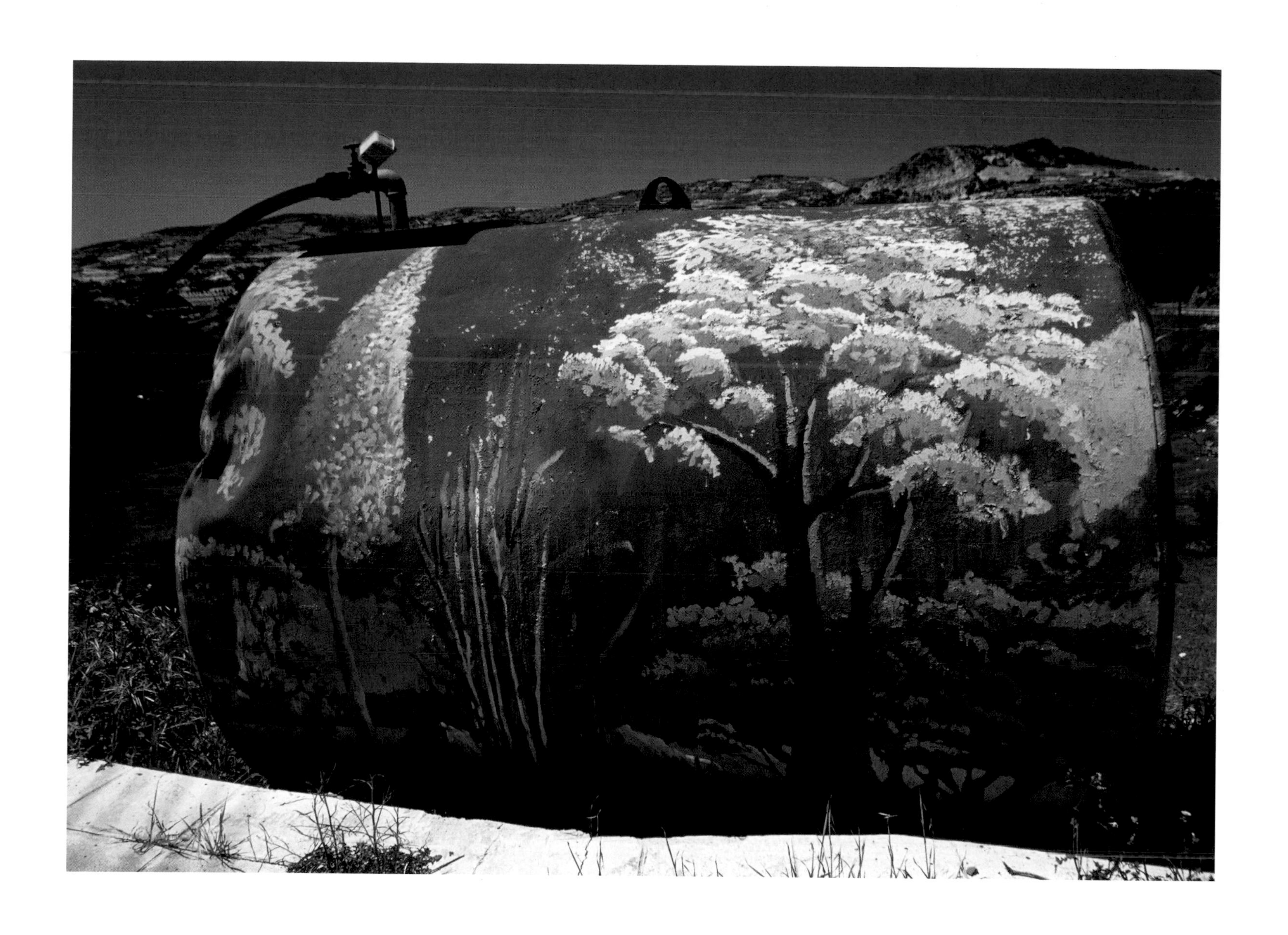

A painted roadside oil drum in the Diarizos Valley, which winds across the southwestern edge of Cyprus.

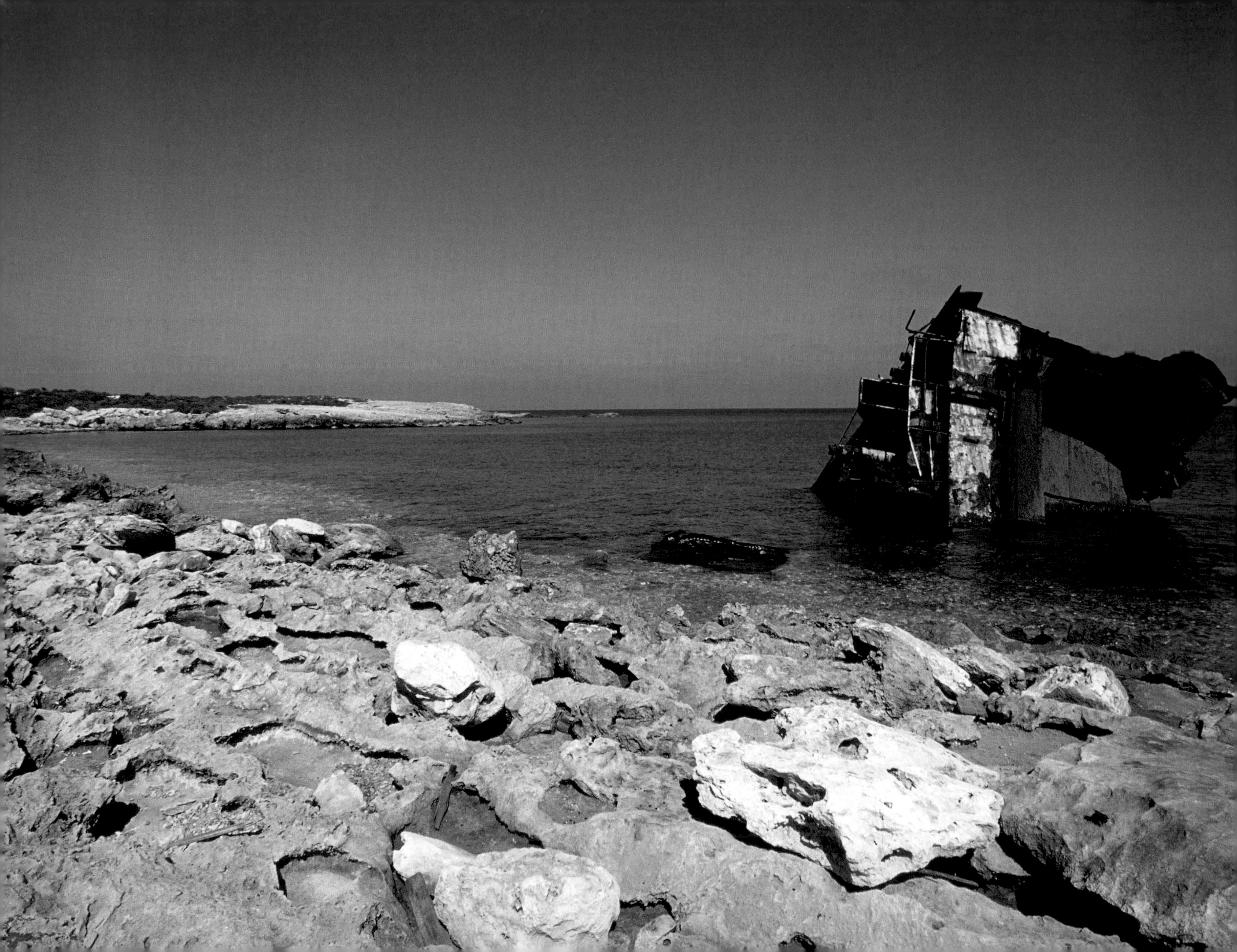

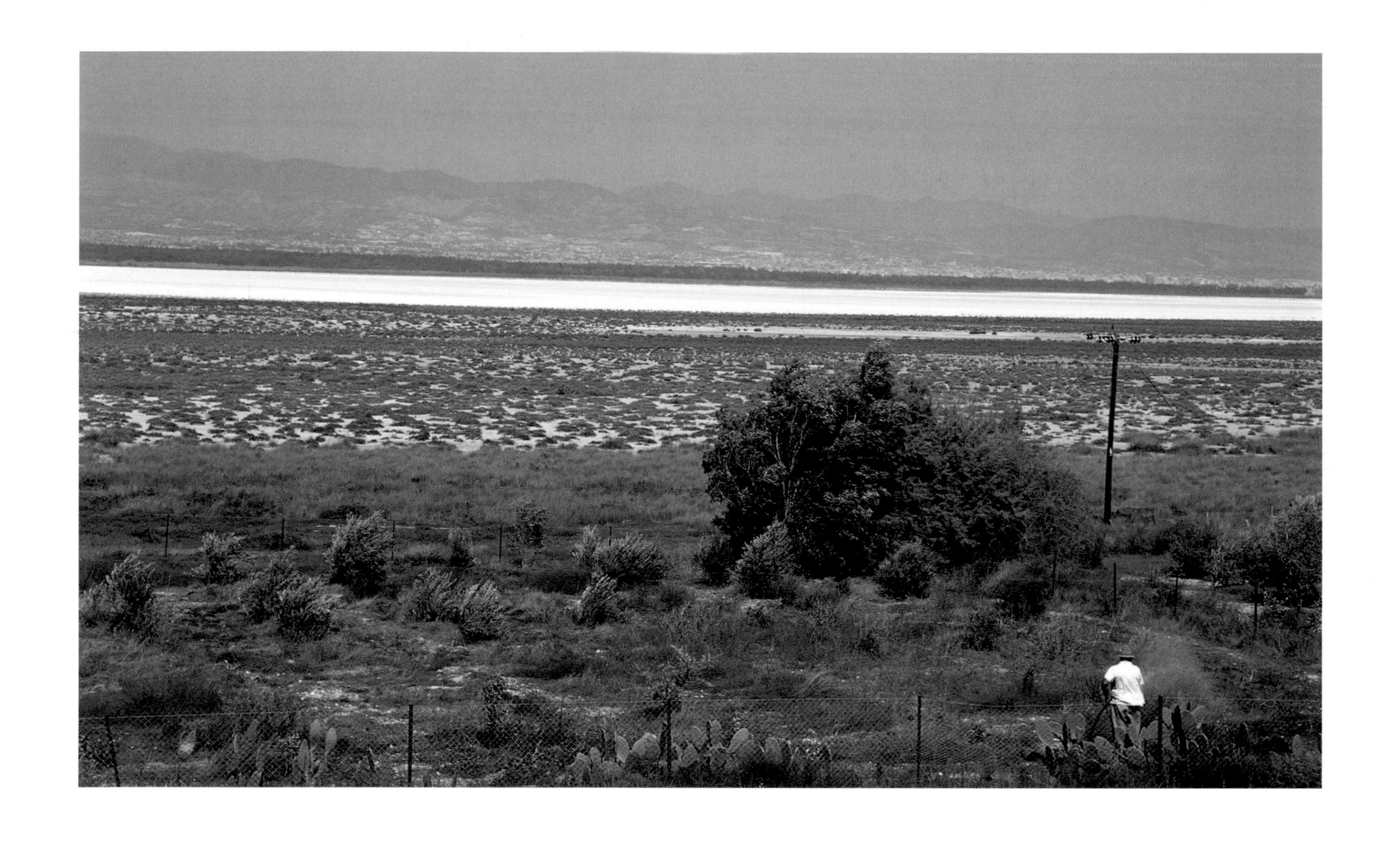

Scrub fringes the low-lying waters of the marsh-bound Salt Lake, situated on the flat Akrotiri Peninsula.
Opposite: The rusting hulk of a wrecked ship rises from the deep blue waters of the Mediterranean. This beach, strewn with puckered and eroded limestone rocks, is on the Akamas Peninsula in western Cyprus.

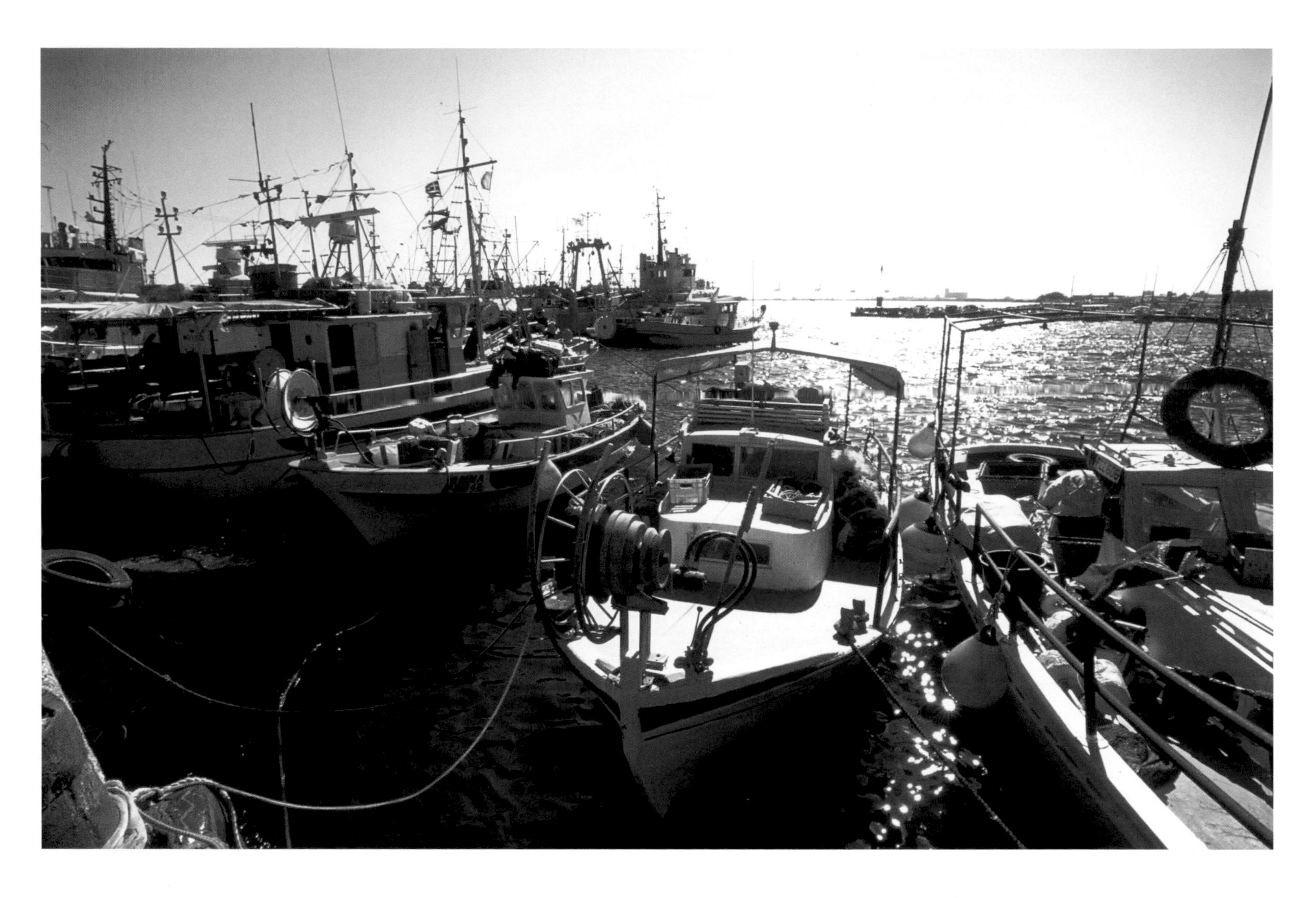

Massed boats of the fishing fleet tied up in the harbour at Limassol, on the southern coast of Cyprus.

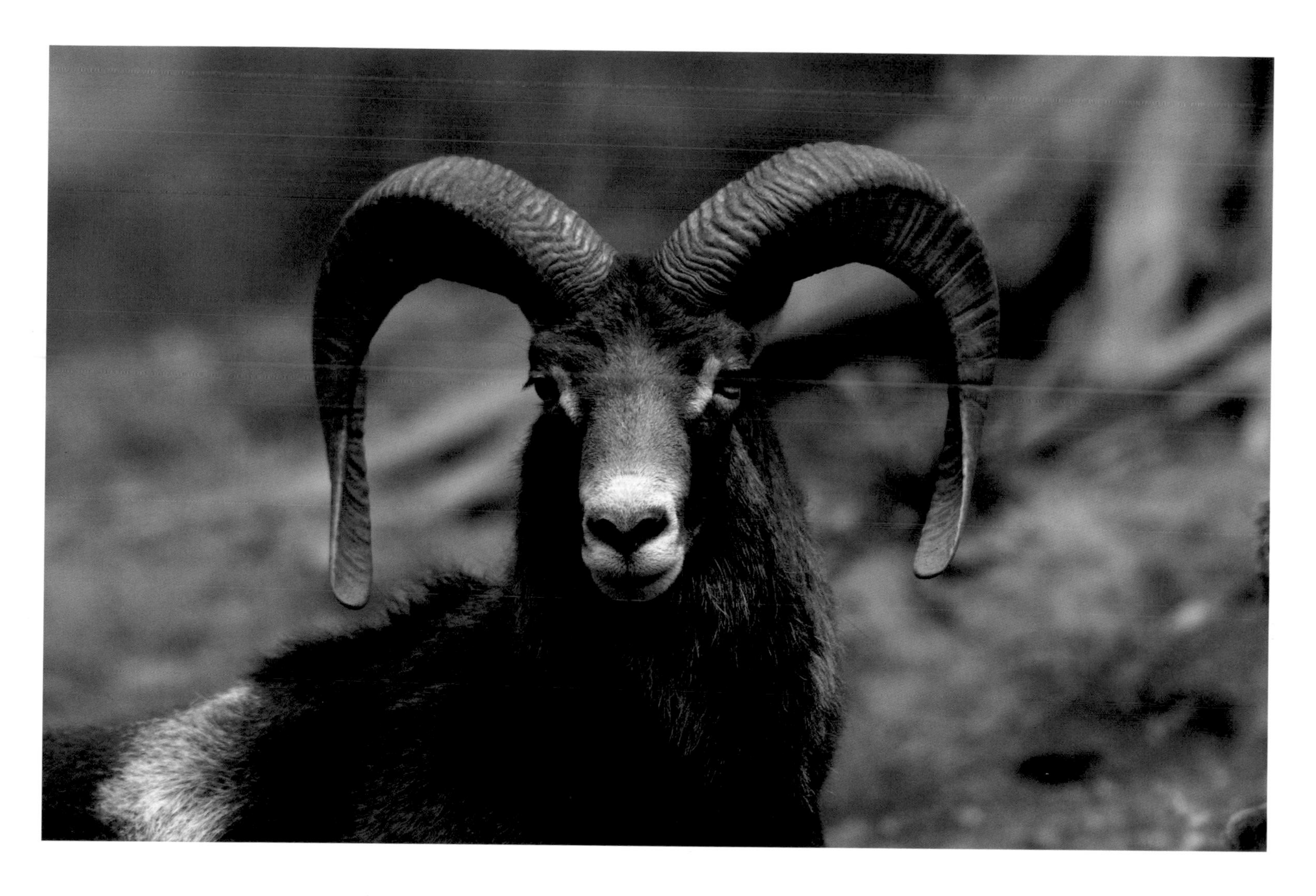

Mouflon sheep live in the grassy plain and mountain regions of Cyprus.

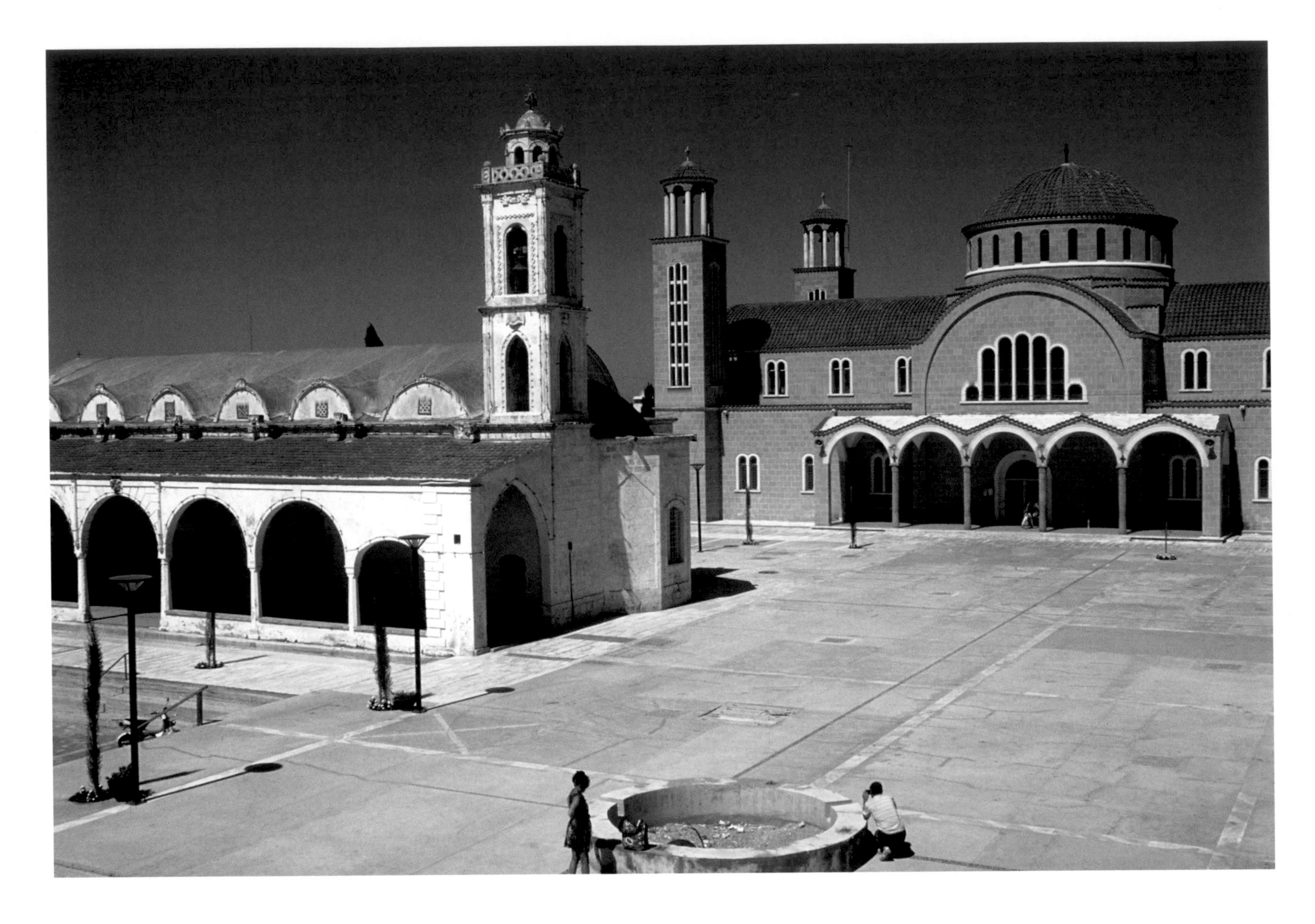

The old church of the Panagia, in Paralimni, is watched over by its more modern counterpart.

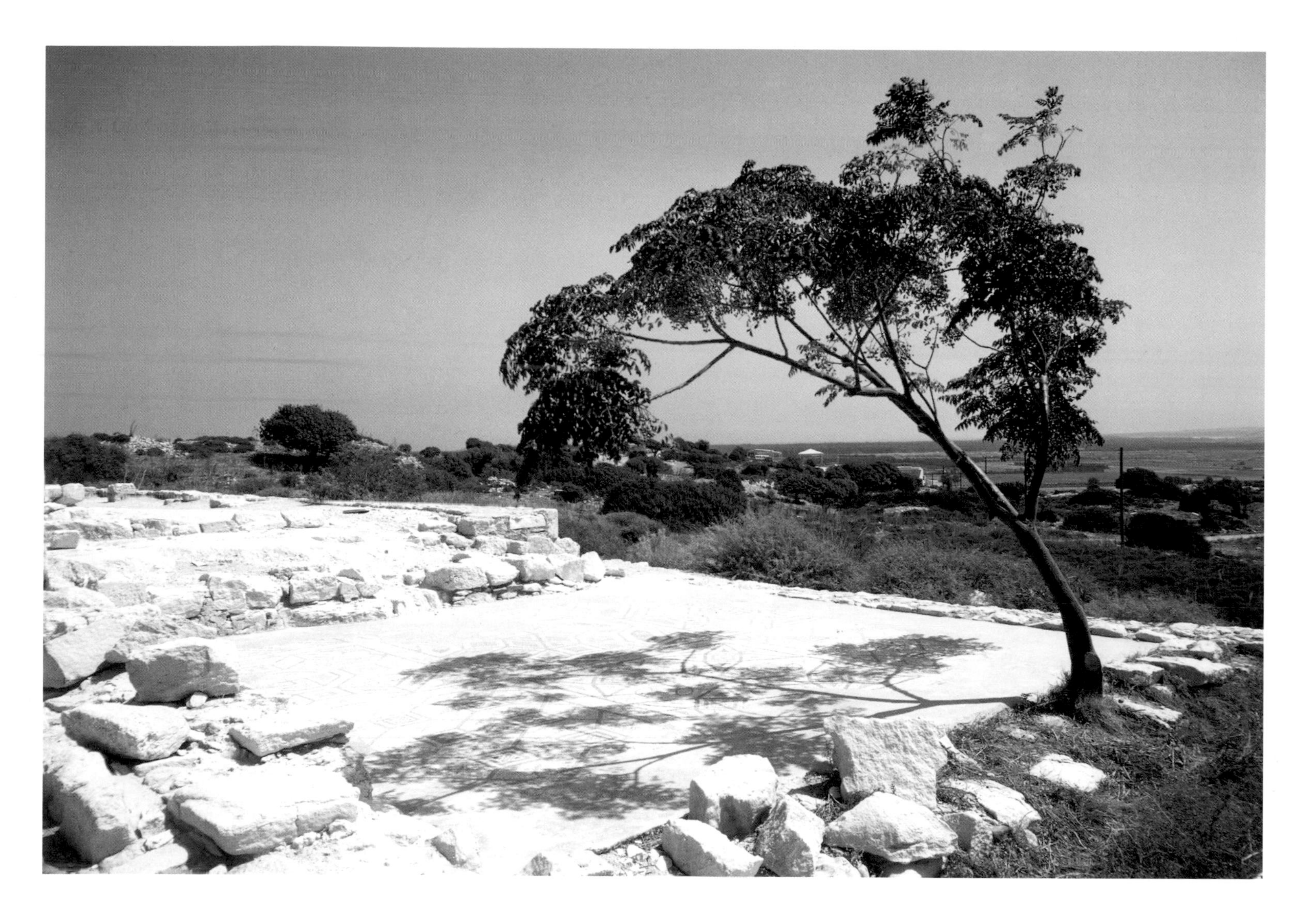

A tree hangs over the remains of a mosaic floor among the ruins of the ancient city of Kourion, perched on an escarpment overlooking the flat Akrotiri Peninsula.

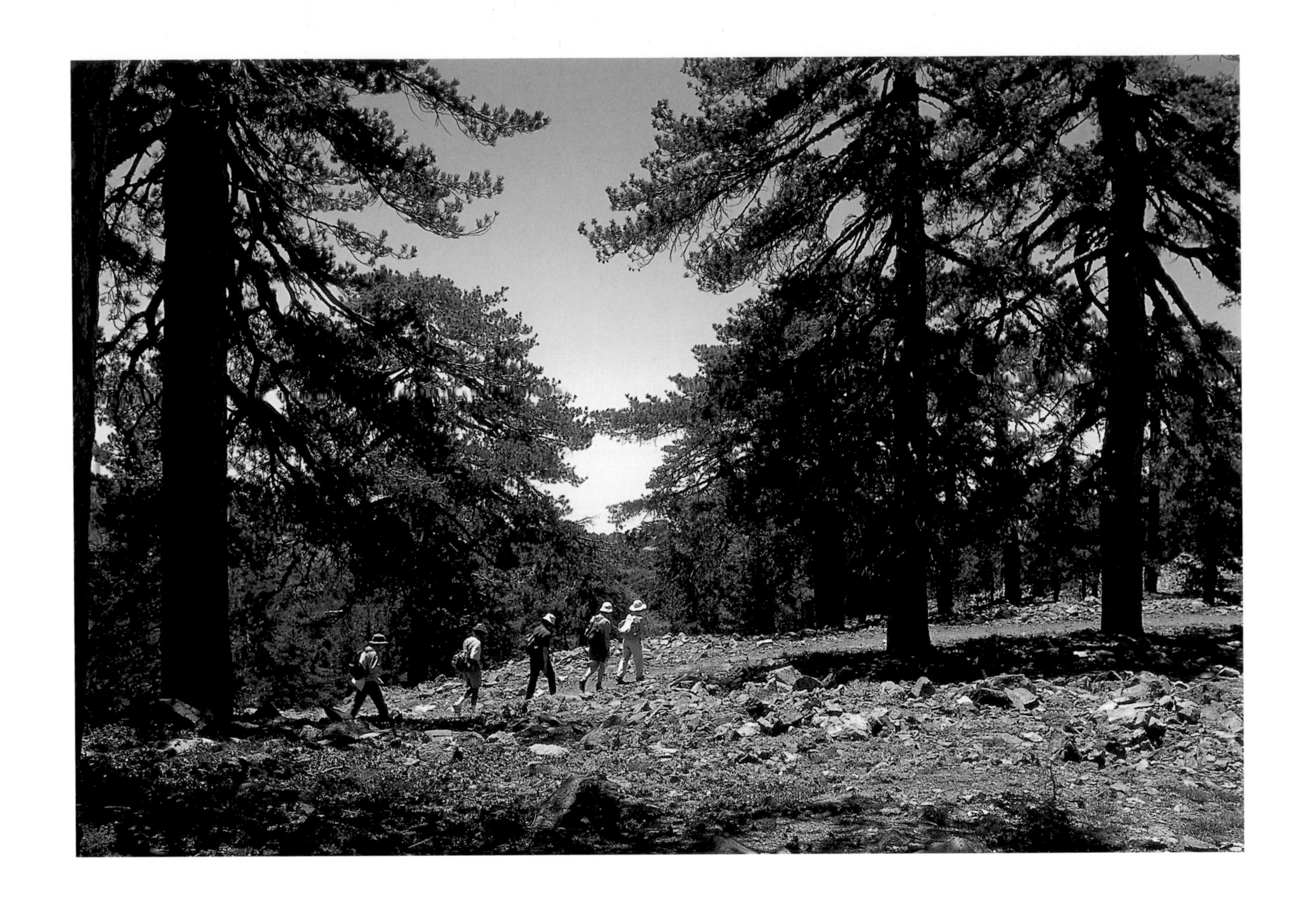

A group of hikers make their way across the stony terrain of the forests of the Troodos Mountains.

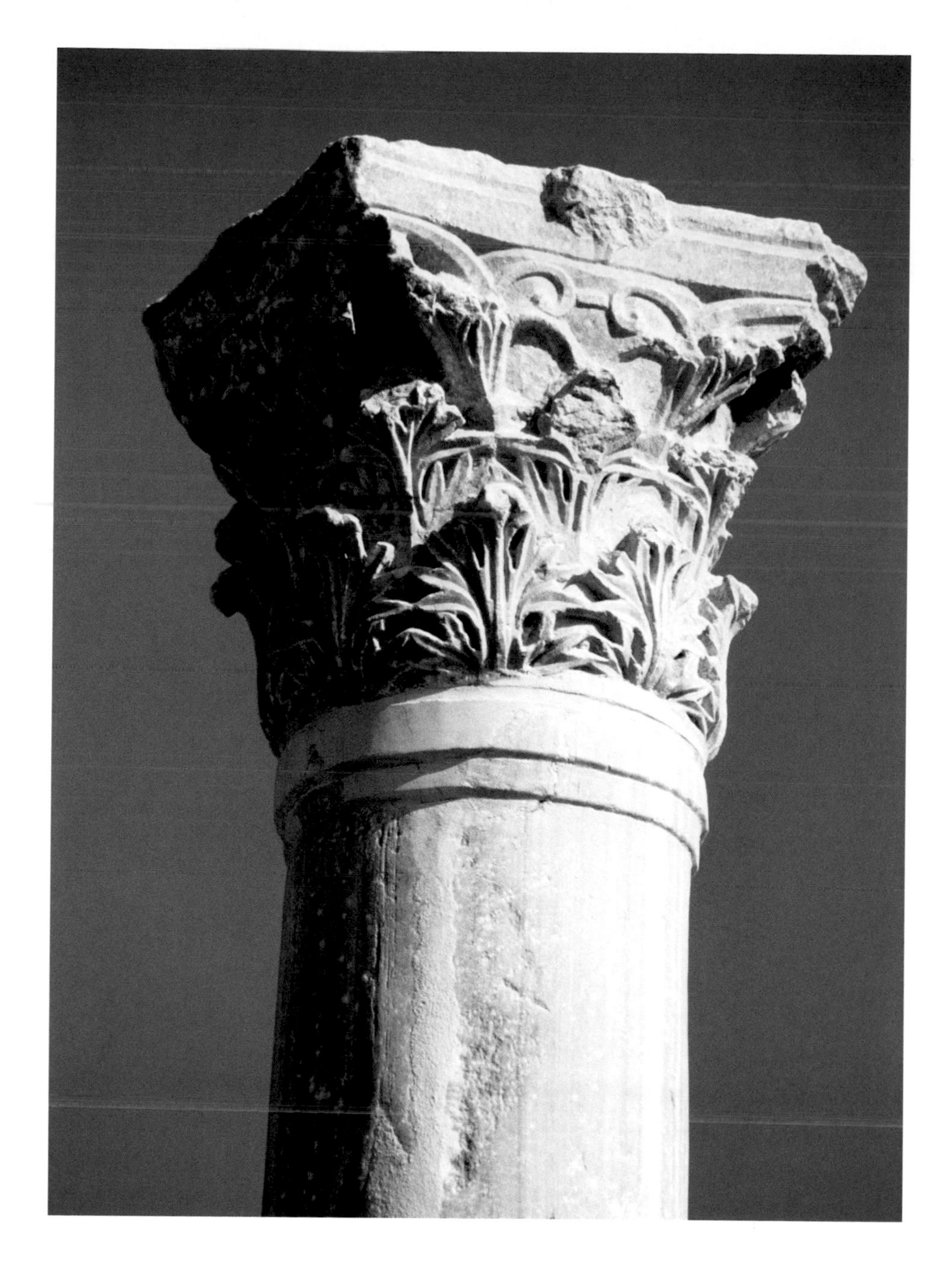

A column topped with a floral capital in the ruins of the city of Kourion on Episkopi Bay, southern Cyprus.

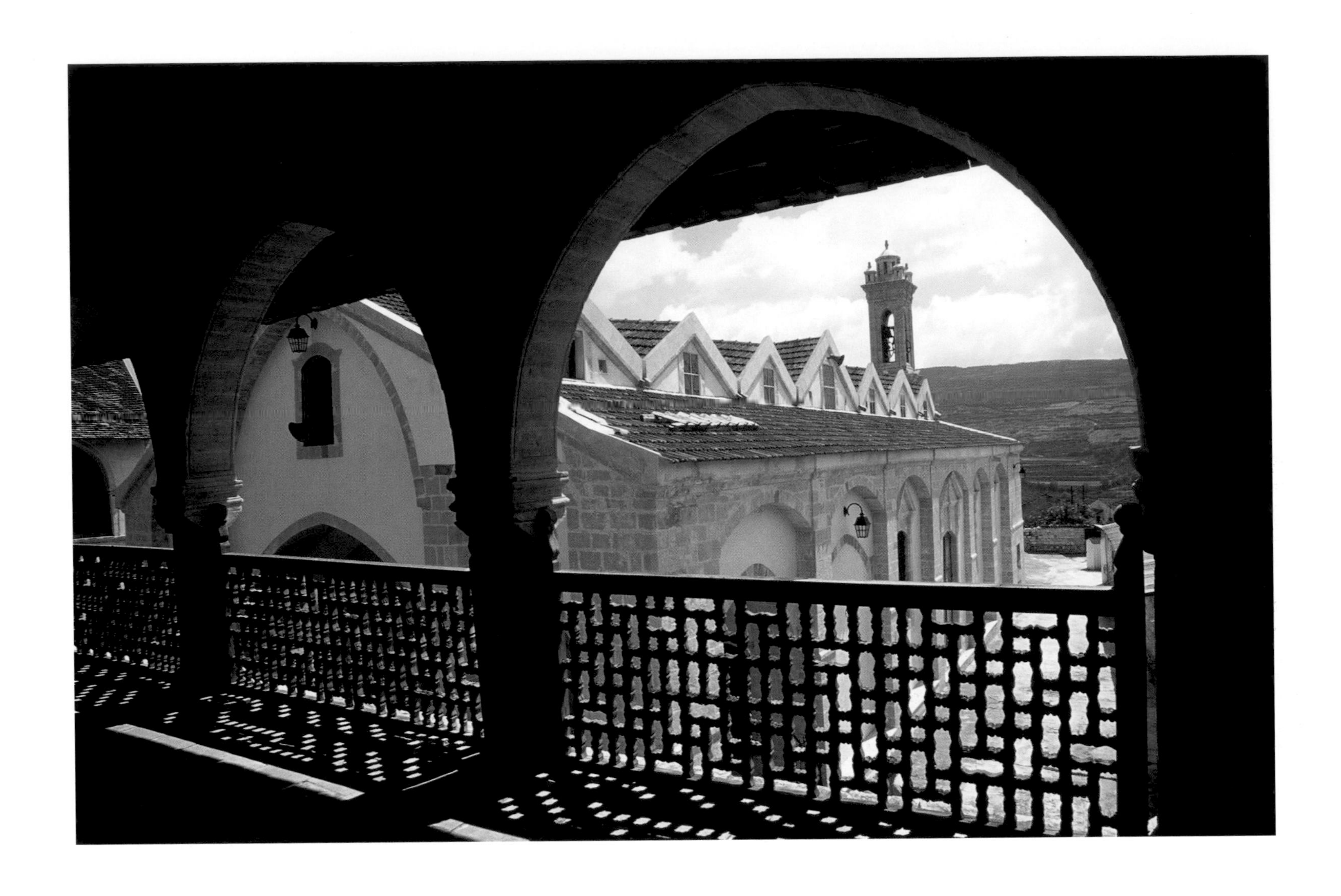

The renovated Holy Cross monastery at Omodos, a village in the Troodos Mountains.

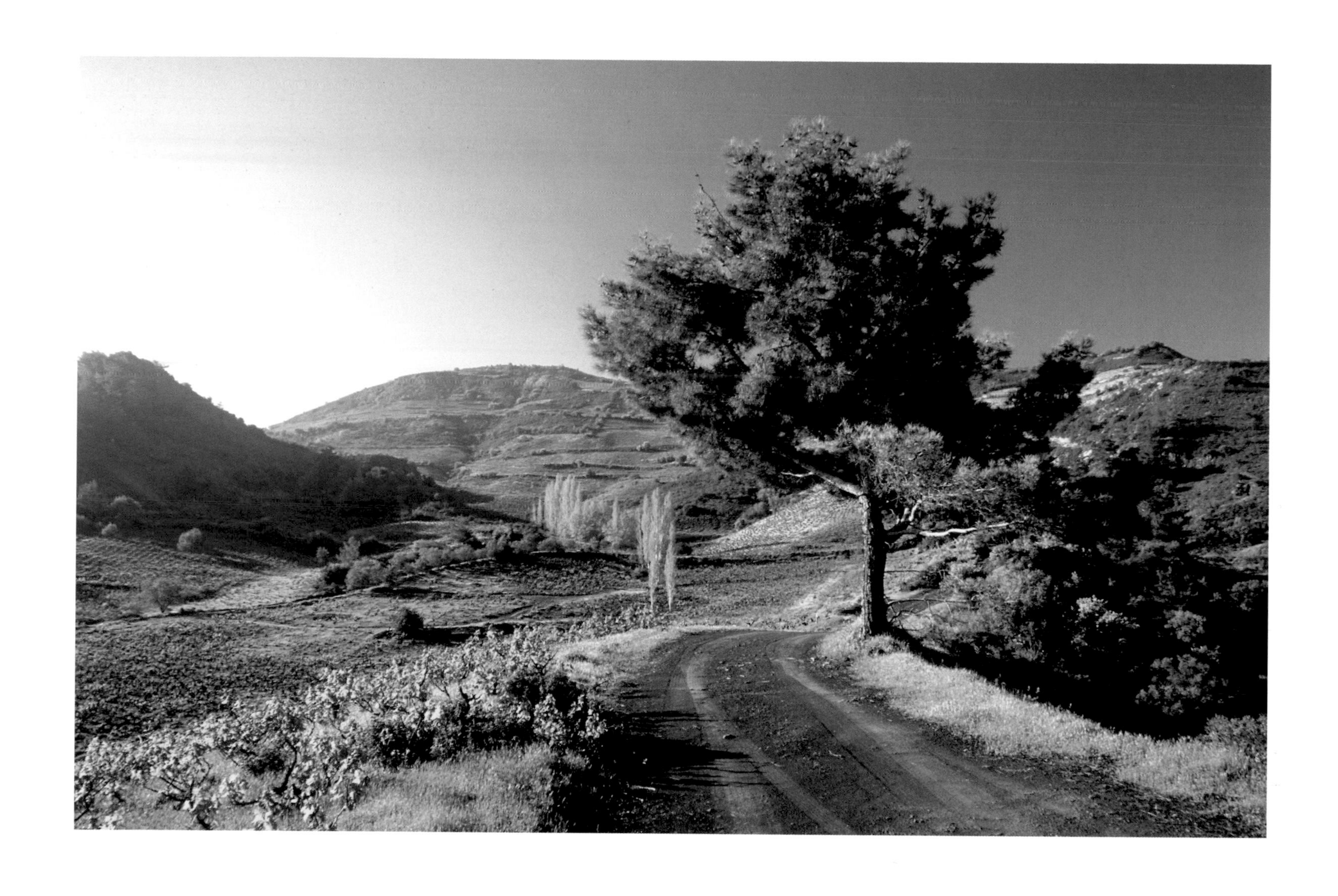

A landscape in the Diarizos Valley, on the way to Troodos.

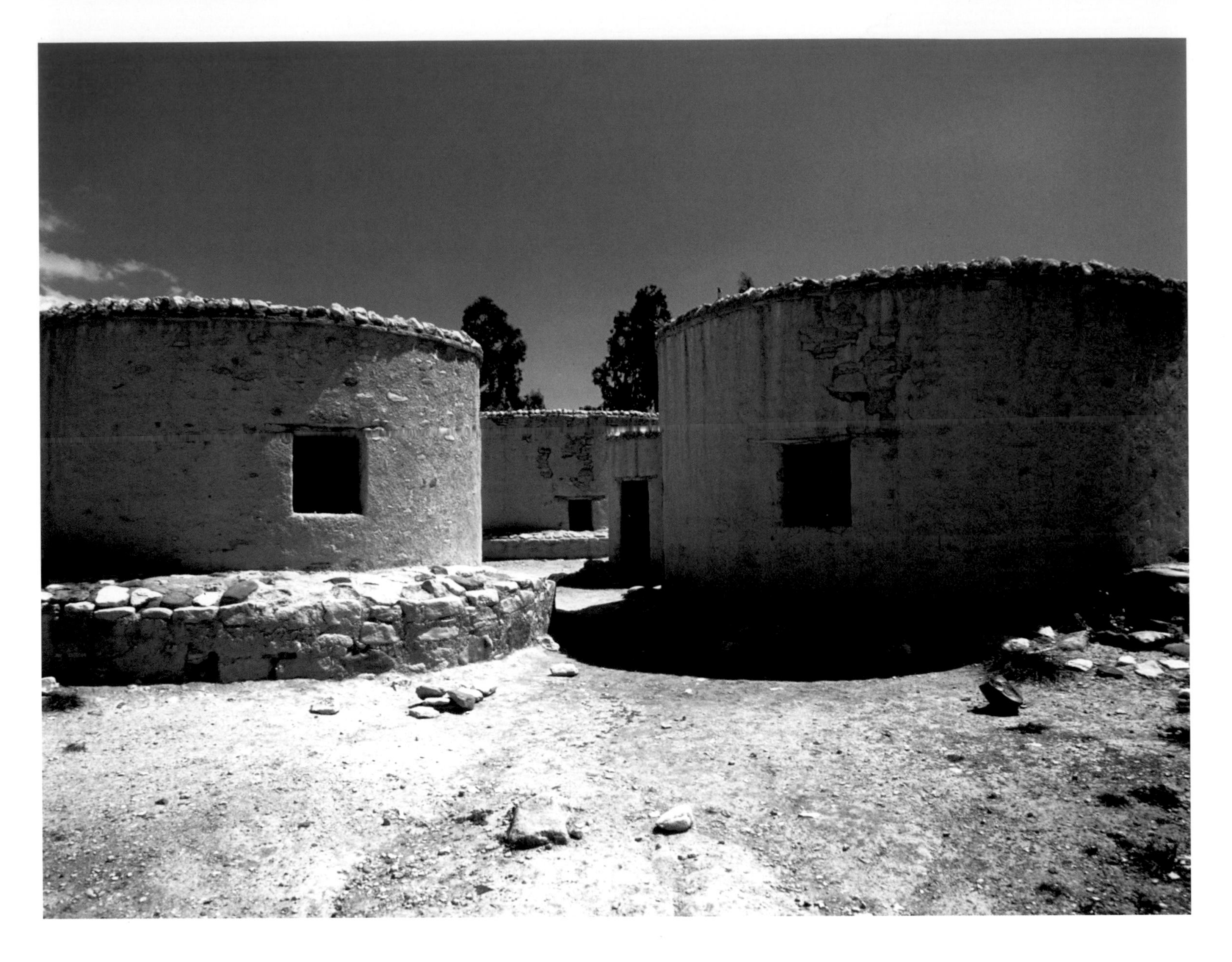

Resconstructed dwellings at the Neolithic village of Choirokoitia, a UNESCO World Cultural Heritage Site.

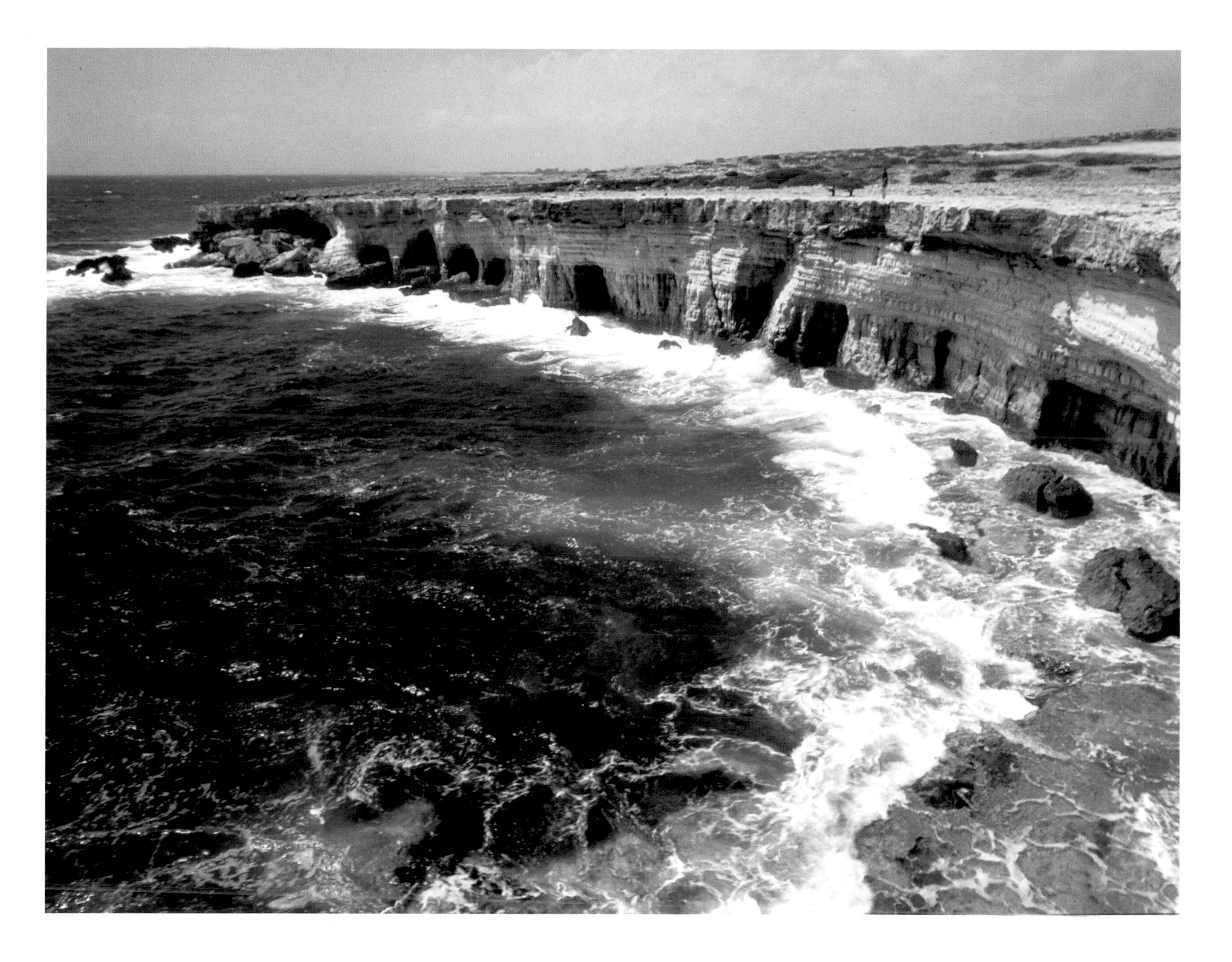

The sea has eroded many caves in the rock face at Cape Gkreko.

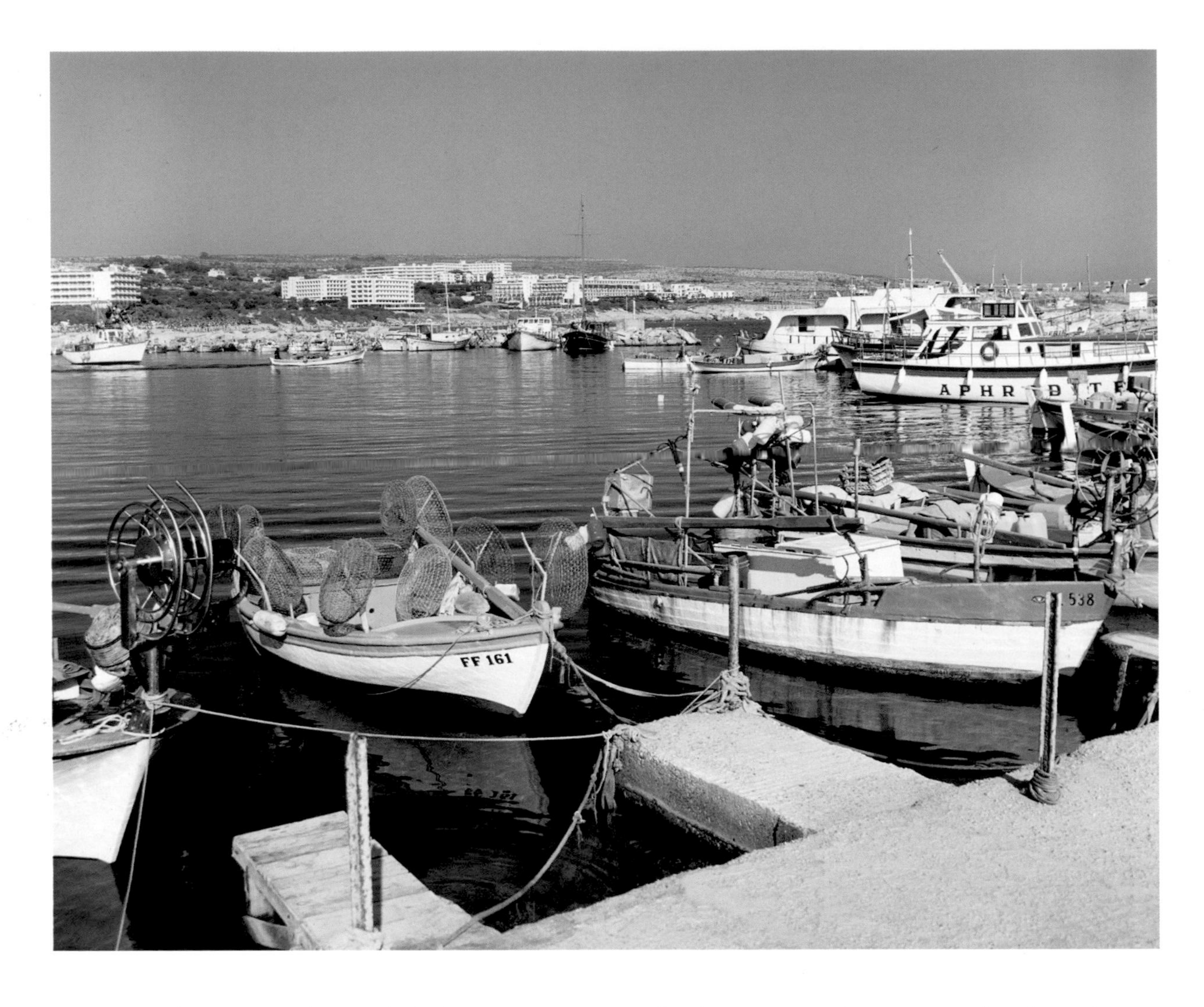

A line of fishing boats tied up in the harbour at Agia Napa, a florishing resort on the east coast of southern Cyprus.

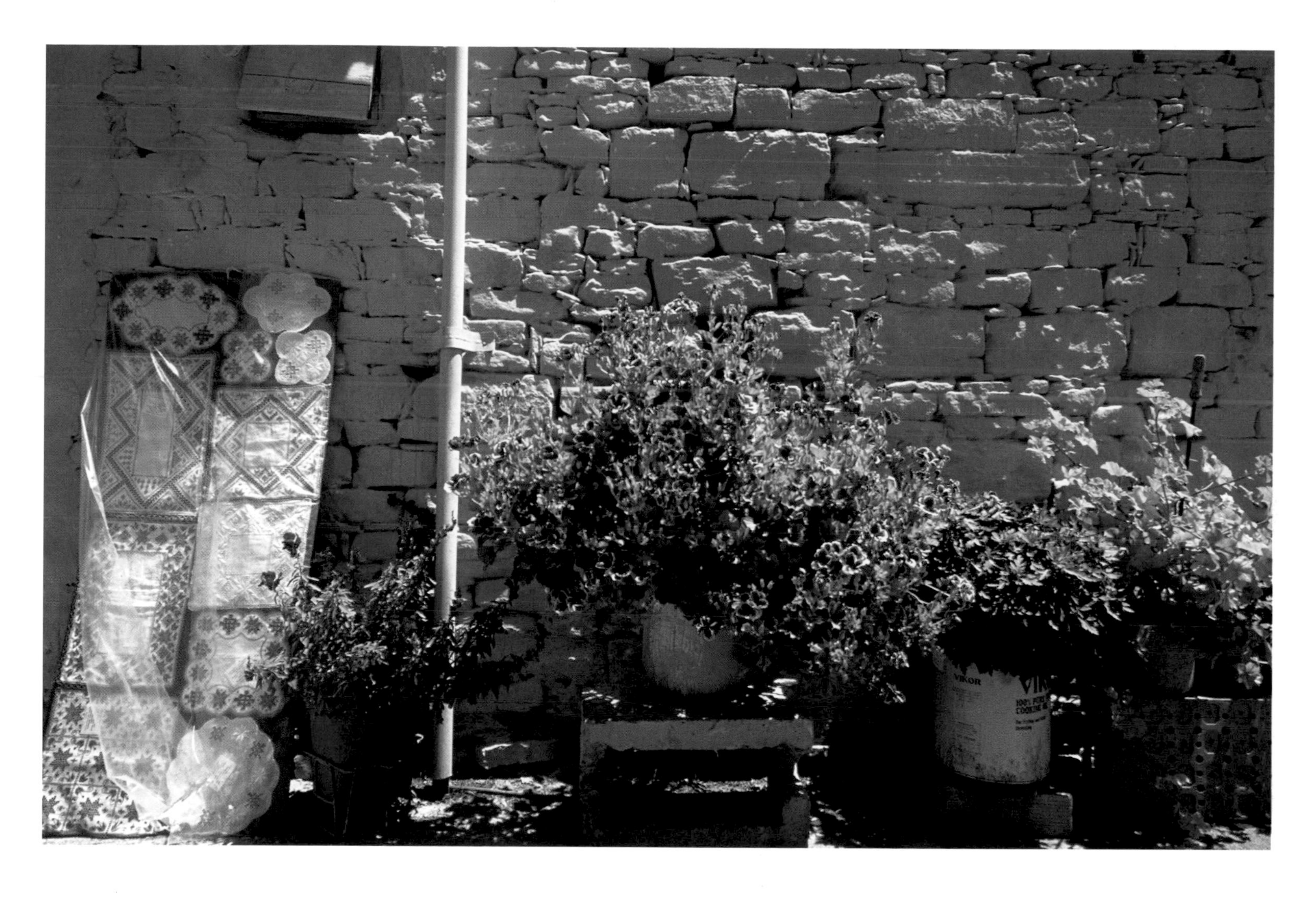

Samples of lace add to this charming display of colour set against a whitewashed stone wall.

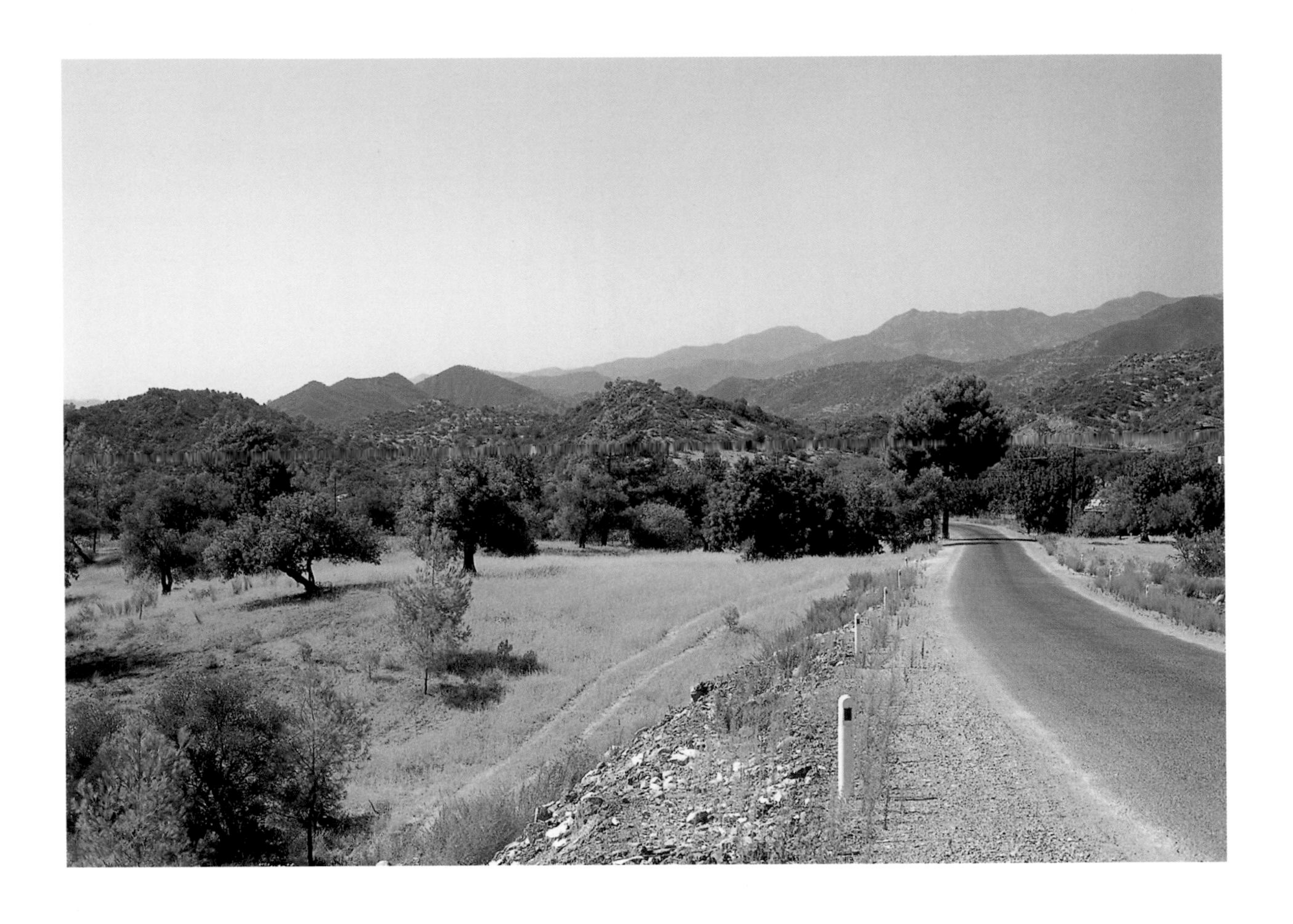

A narrow road winds its way towards the Troodos Mountains which dominate the entire southwest of the island.

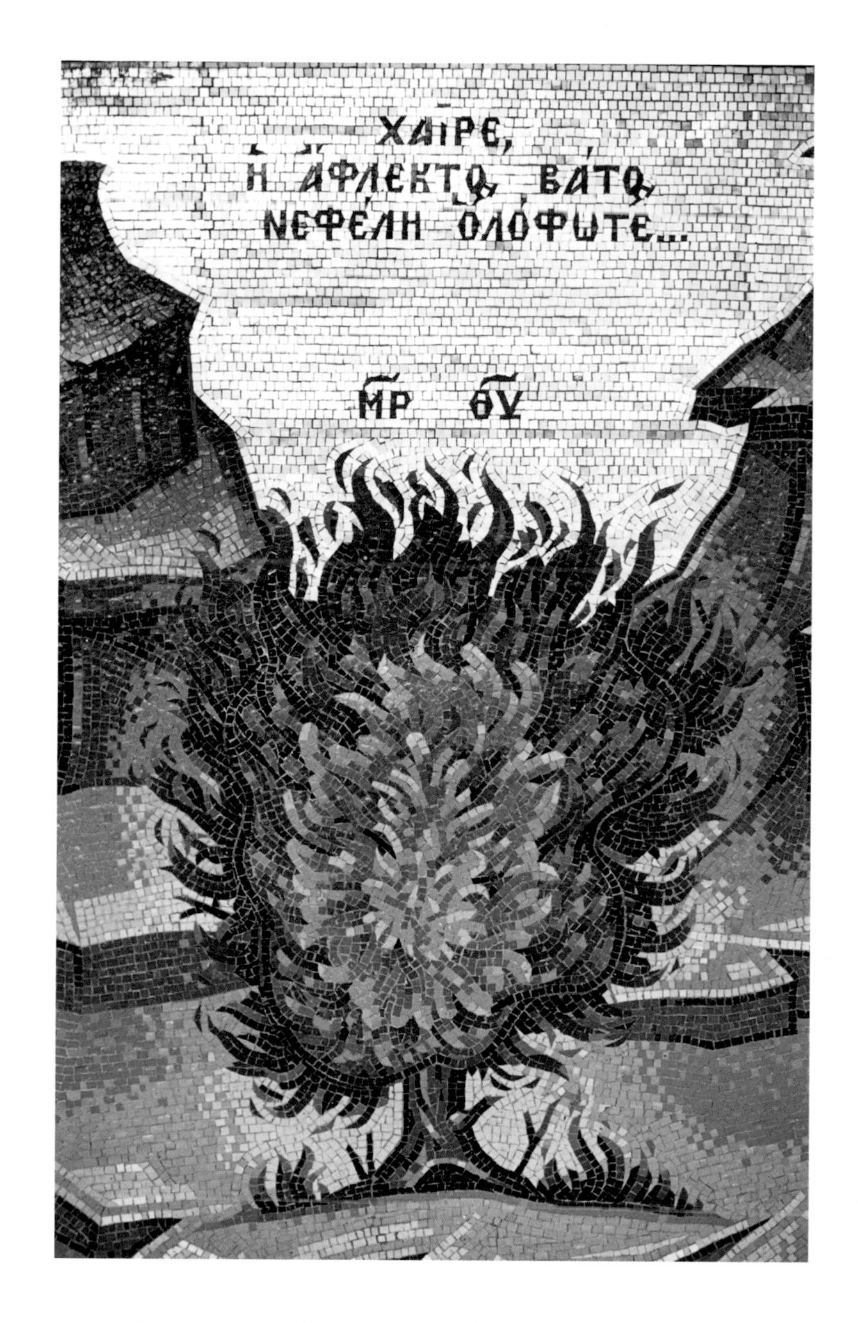

A mosaic at Kykkos Monastery, depicting the burning bush that Moses encounters in the Book of Exodus.

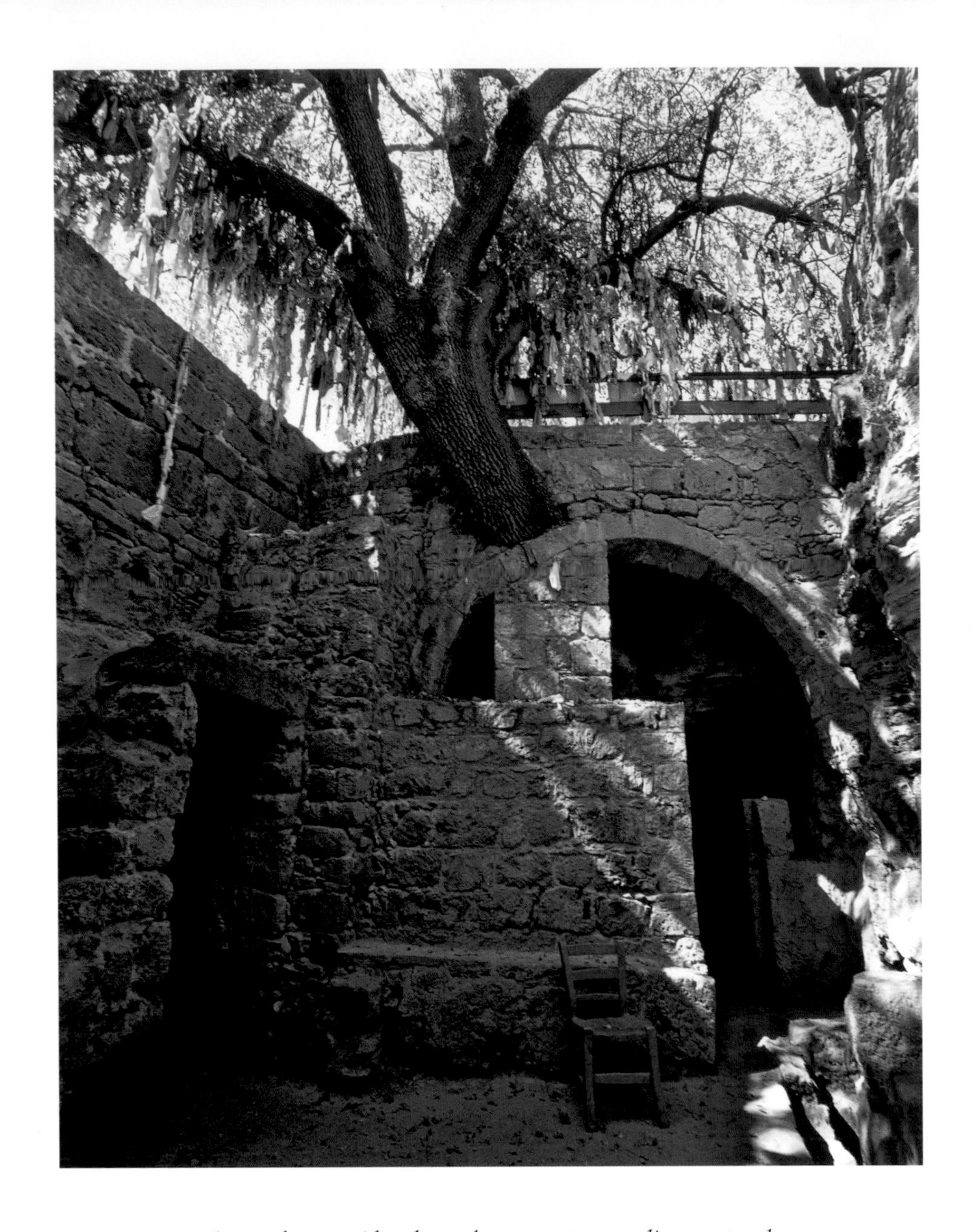

A sacred tree, said to have the power to cure disease, stands near the entrance to the catacomb of Agia Solomoni, Pafos, decked with votive offerings.

A view of the rocky coastline leading to the fishing village of Pomos on the hilly north coast.

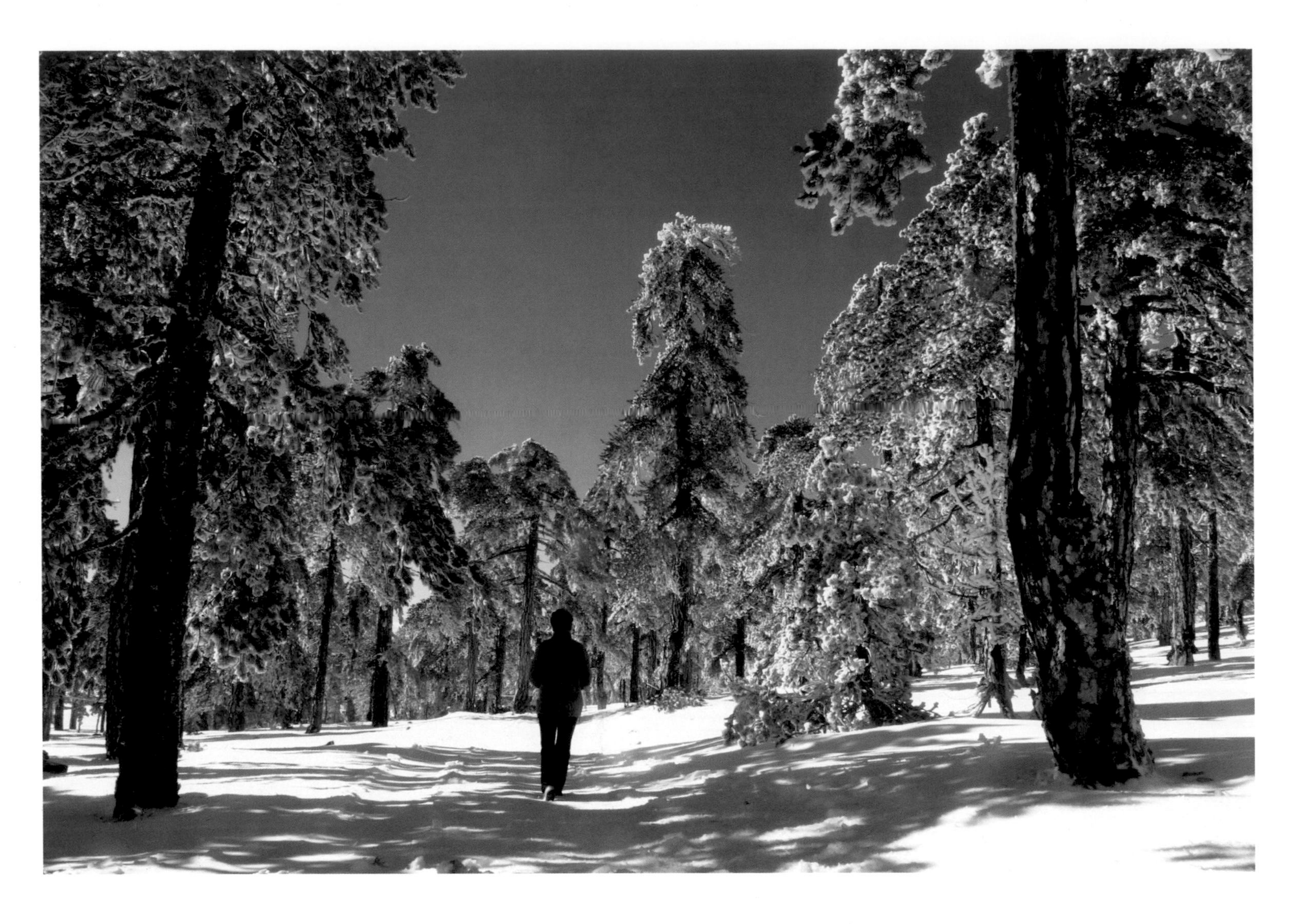

Walking through snow covered pine trees on Mount Olympos.

The blue seas of Limassol are busy with boats large and small.

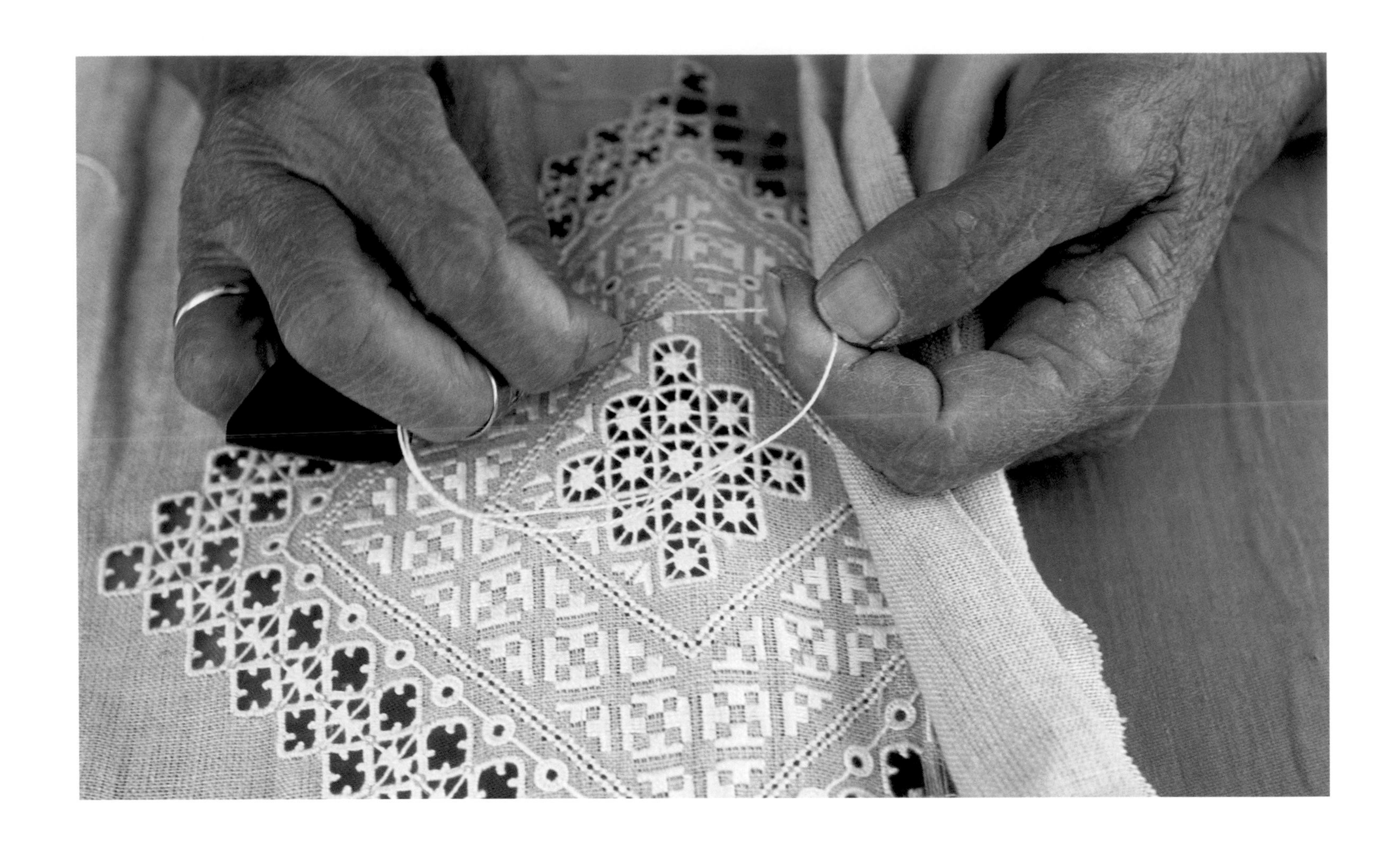

An elderly lace-maker works on a piece of lace in the hill town of Lefkara, in southern Cyprus.

Rocks beneath the surface are clearly visible through the crystal-clear waters off the beach of Kato Pyrgos on the north coast of Cyprus.

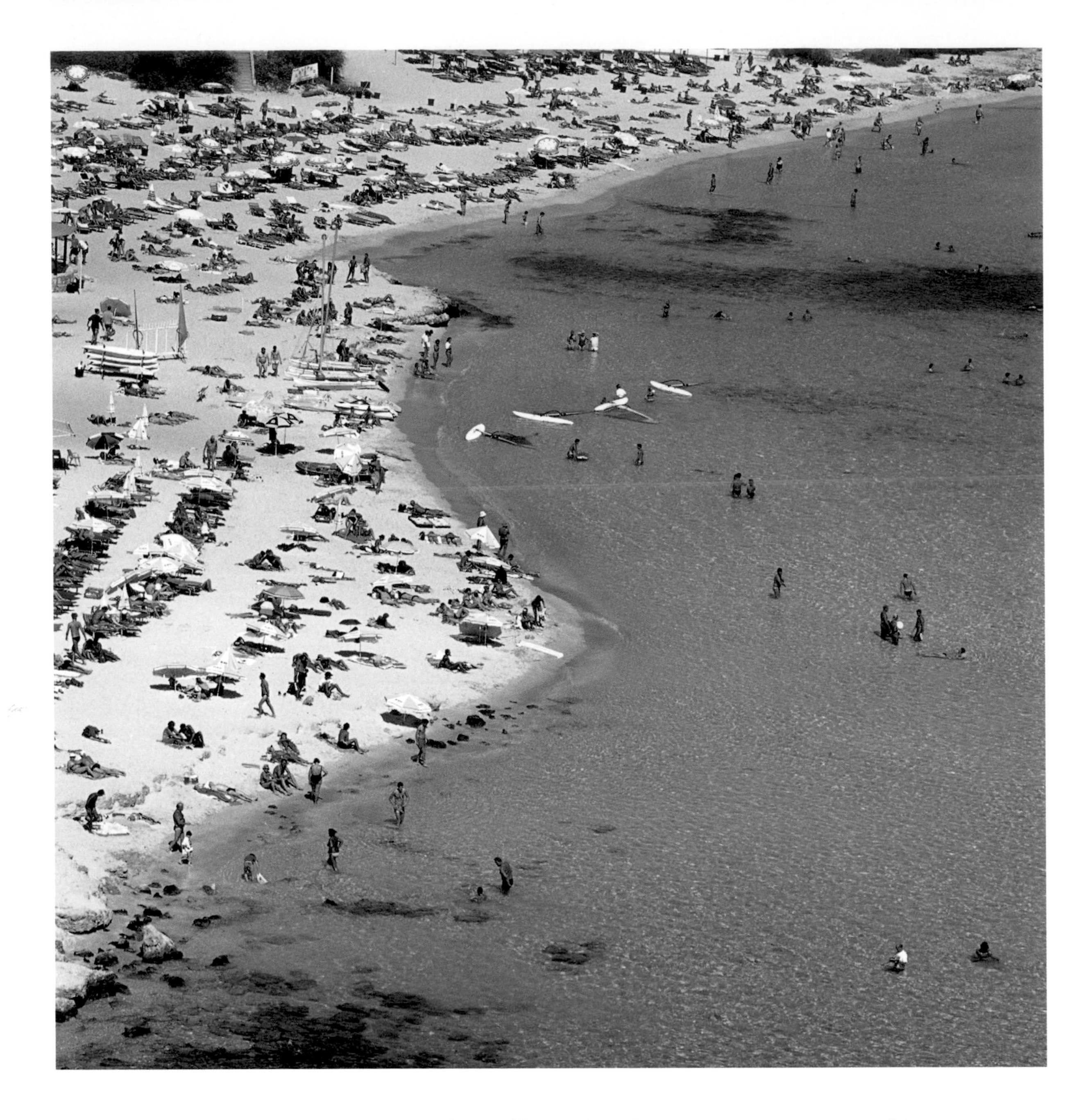

The crowded beach at Nissi Bay, where golden sands and azure waters attract sun-worshippers.

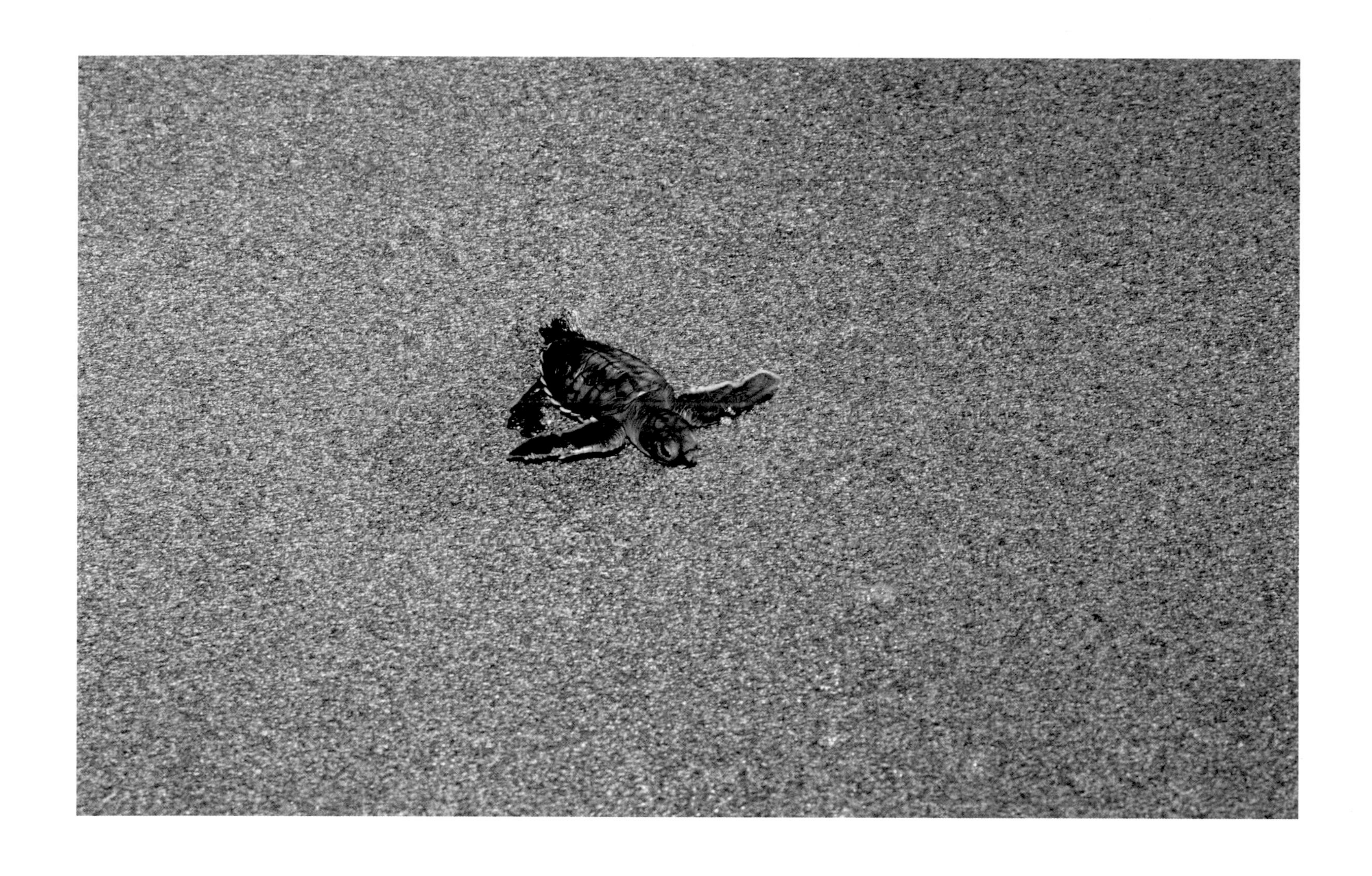

A newly hatched loggerhead turtle makes it way across the sands of Lara Bay to the relative safety of the sea.

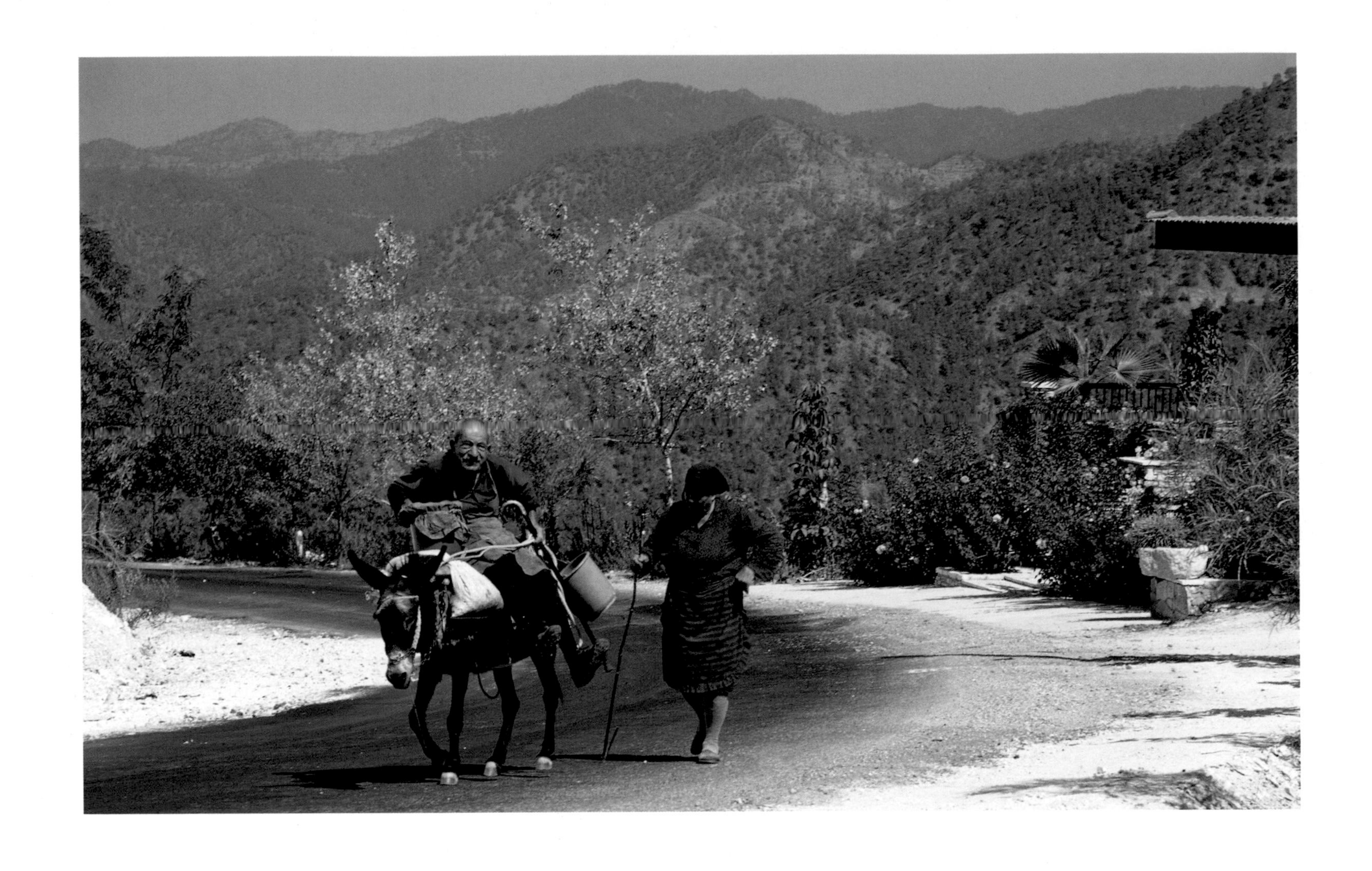

An elderly couple and their heavily laden donkey make their way up a steep mountain road in the forested region of Pano Panagia.
Opposite: A view over the sea from Akamas, the peninsula at the far west of Cyprus.

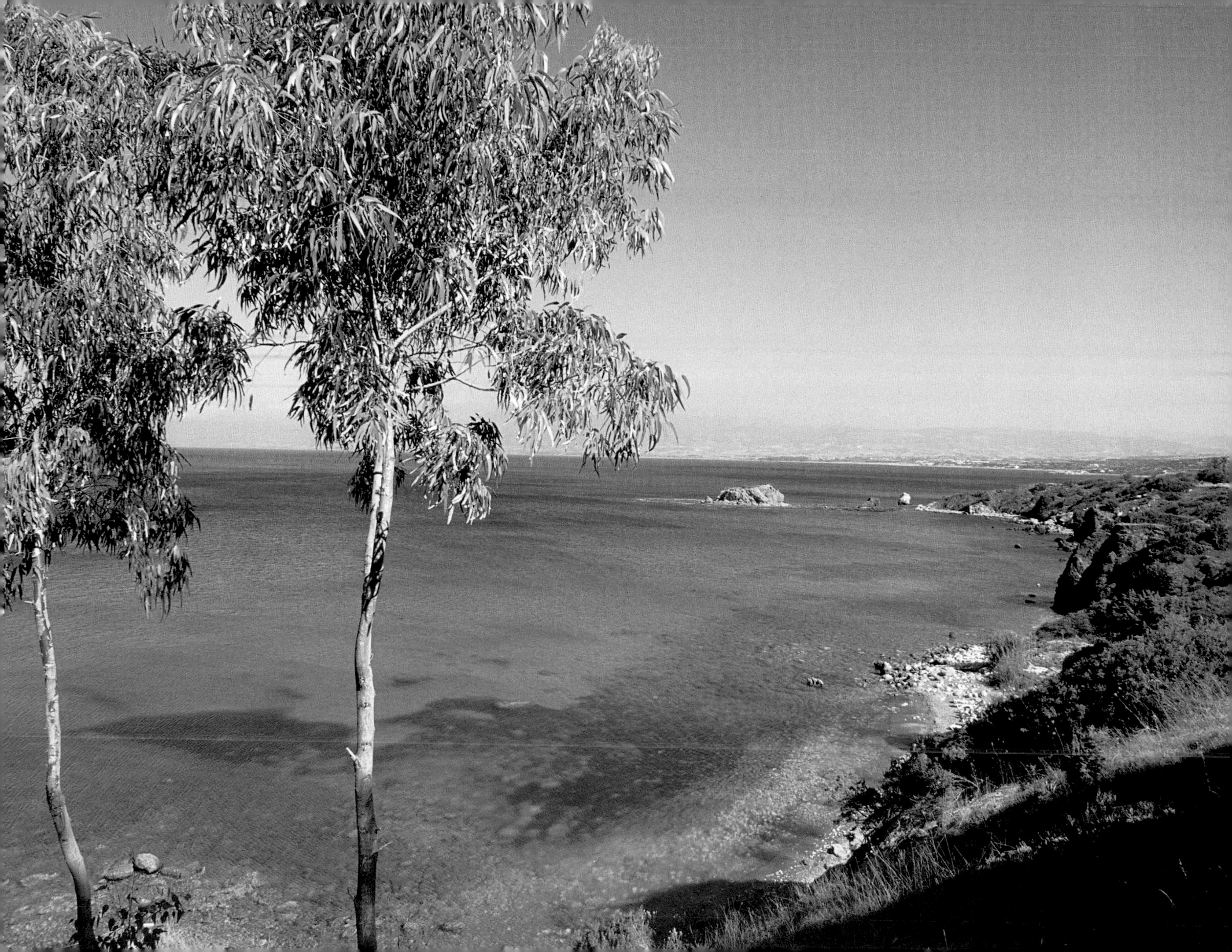

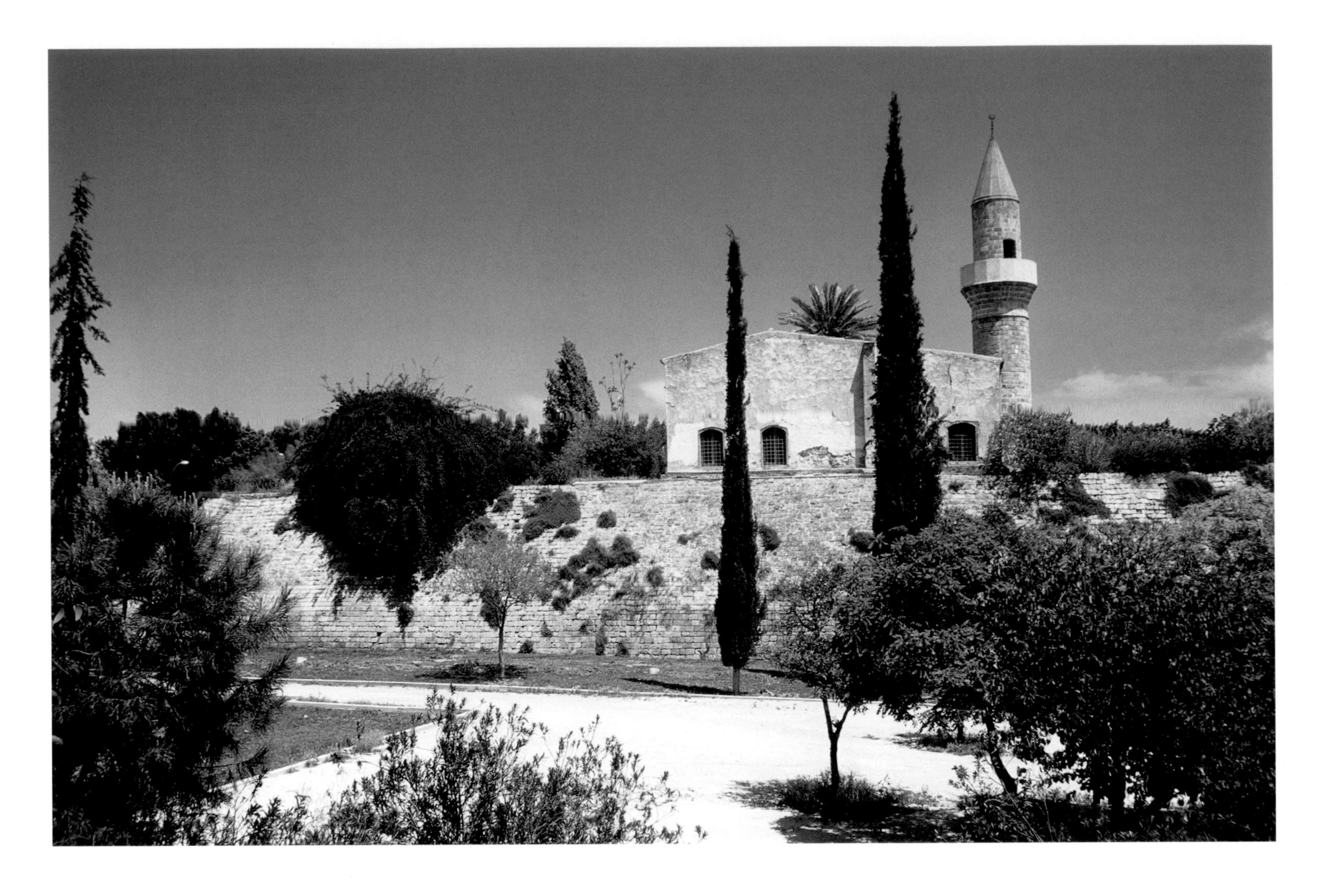

The Venetian walls in Nicosia, with the Bayraktar Mosque in the background.
The mosque, dating from 1820, marks the spot where the Ottomans breached the walls in 1570.

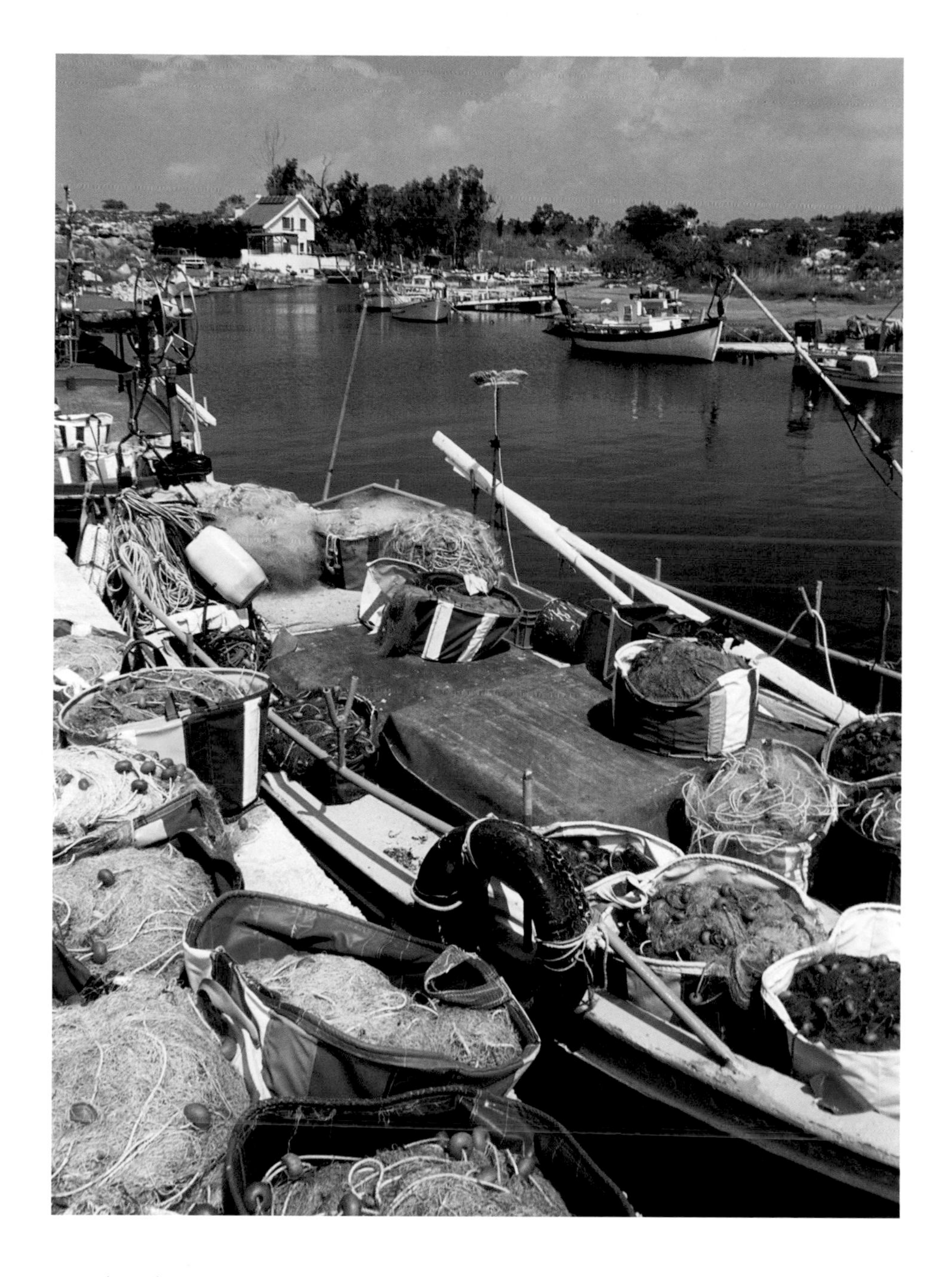

Fishing boats ready to set off from Potamos Harbour, in the eastern Larnaka region.

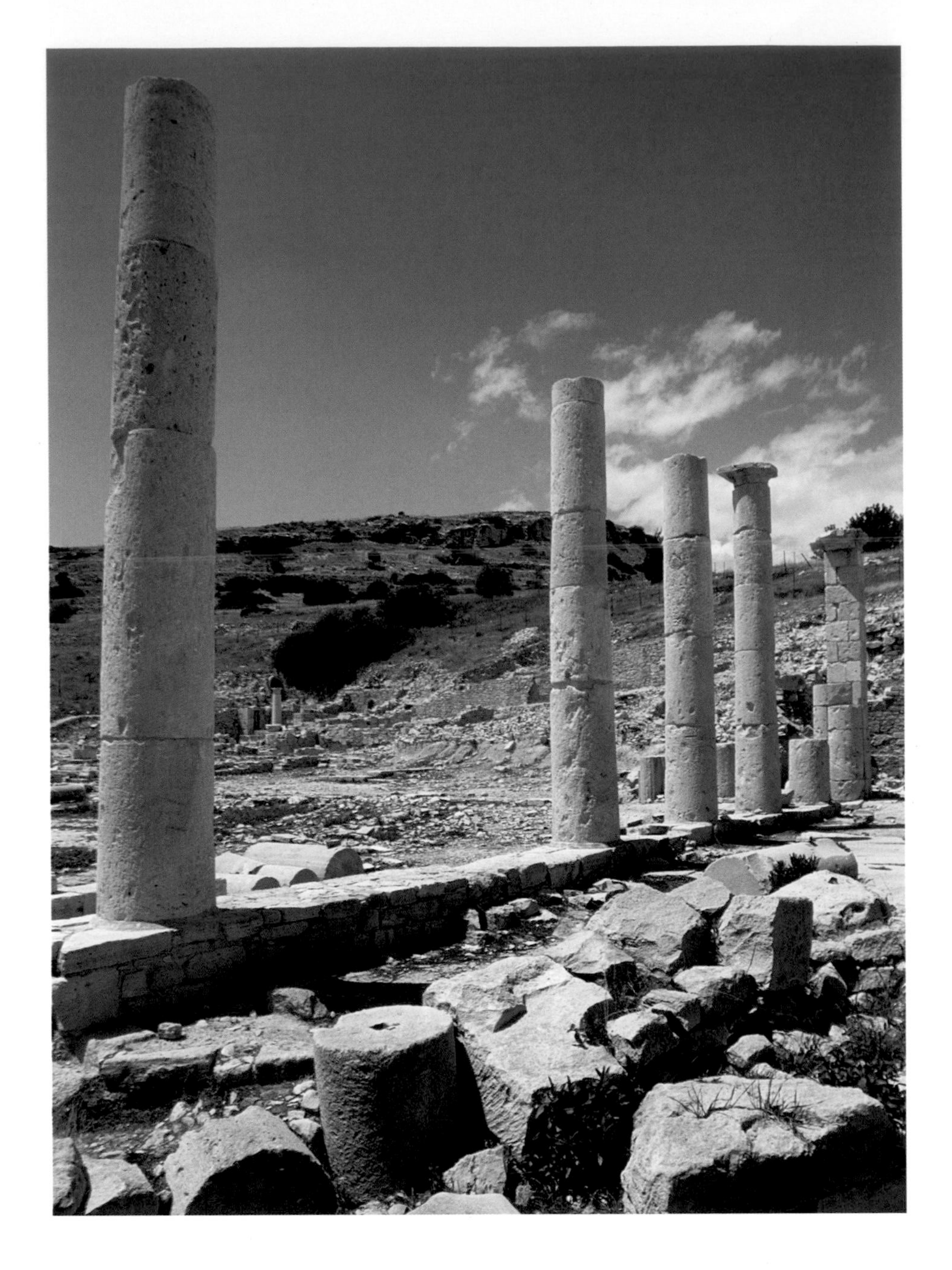

Some of the remains of the ruined city of Amathous, one of the seats of the cult of Aphrodite.

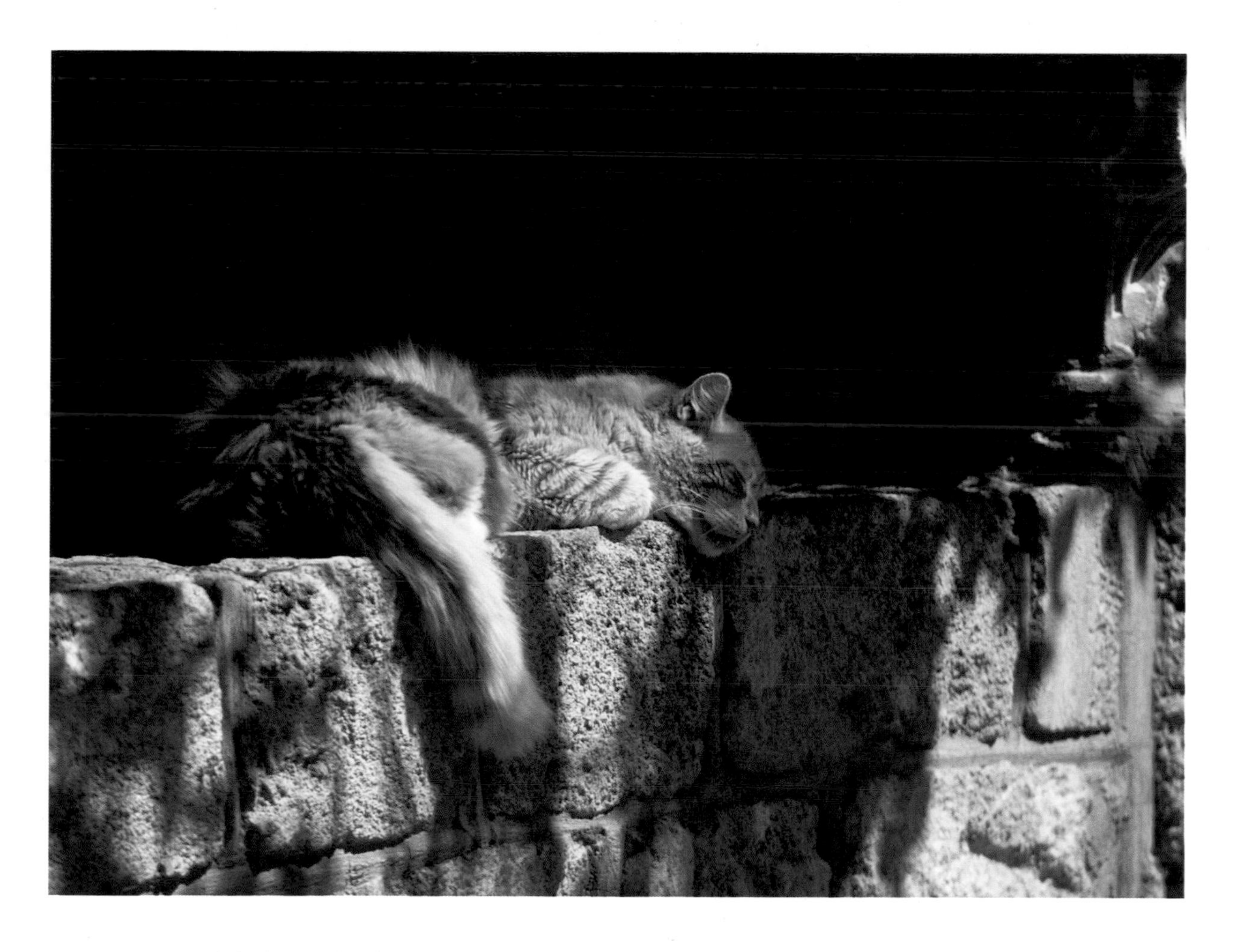

One of the hundreds of cats that enjoy the protection of the convent of Agios Nikolaos ton Gaton (St Nicholas of the Cats) in Limassol. According to legend, St Helena brought the ancestors of the cats to Cyprus to supress the snakes.

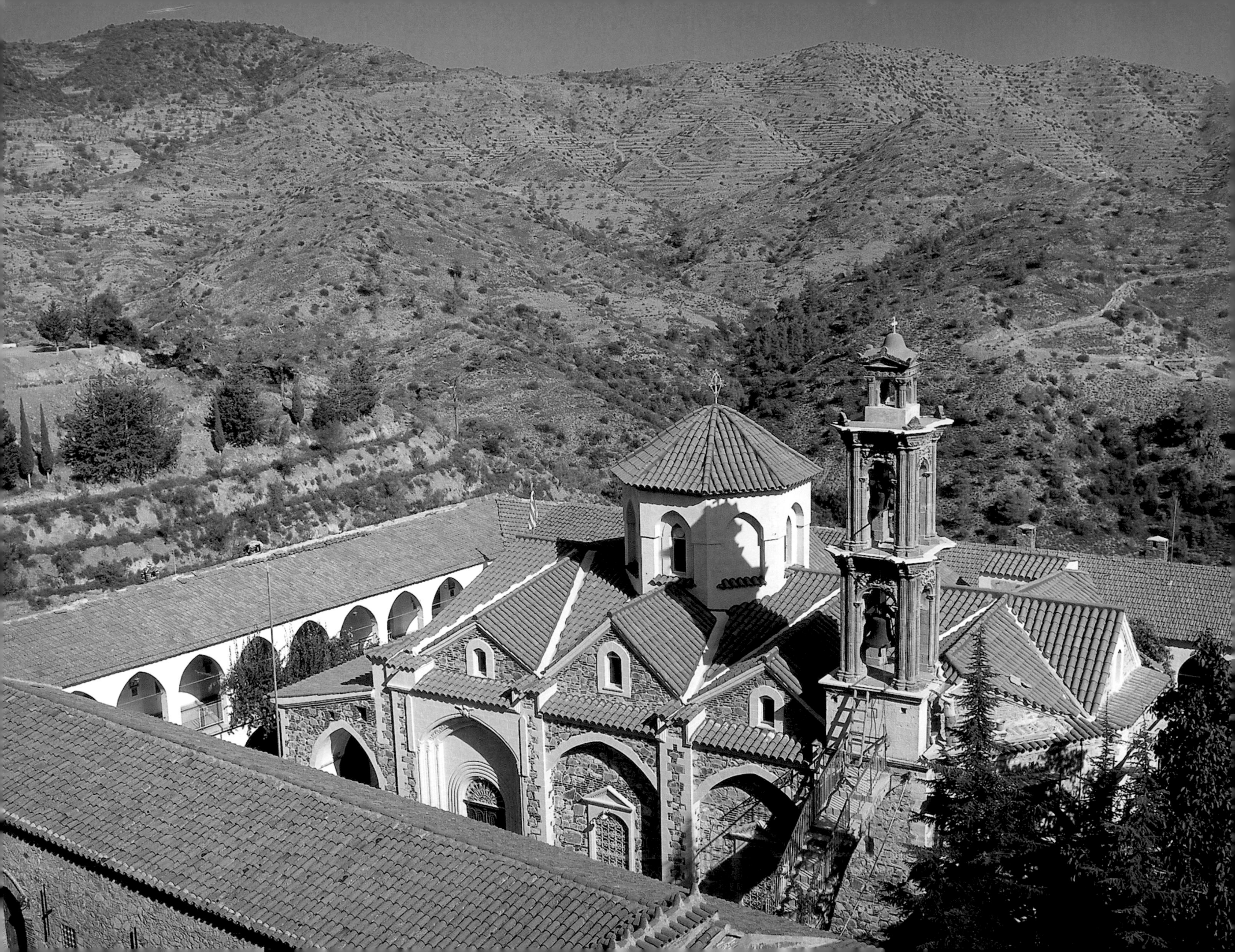

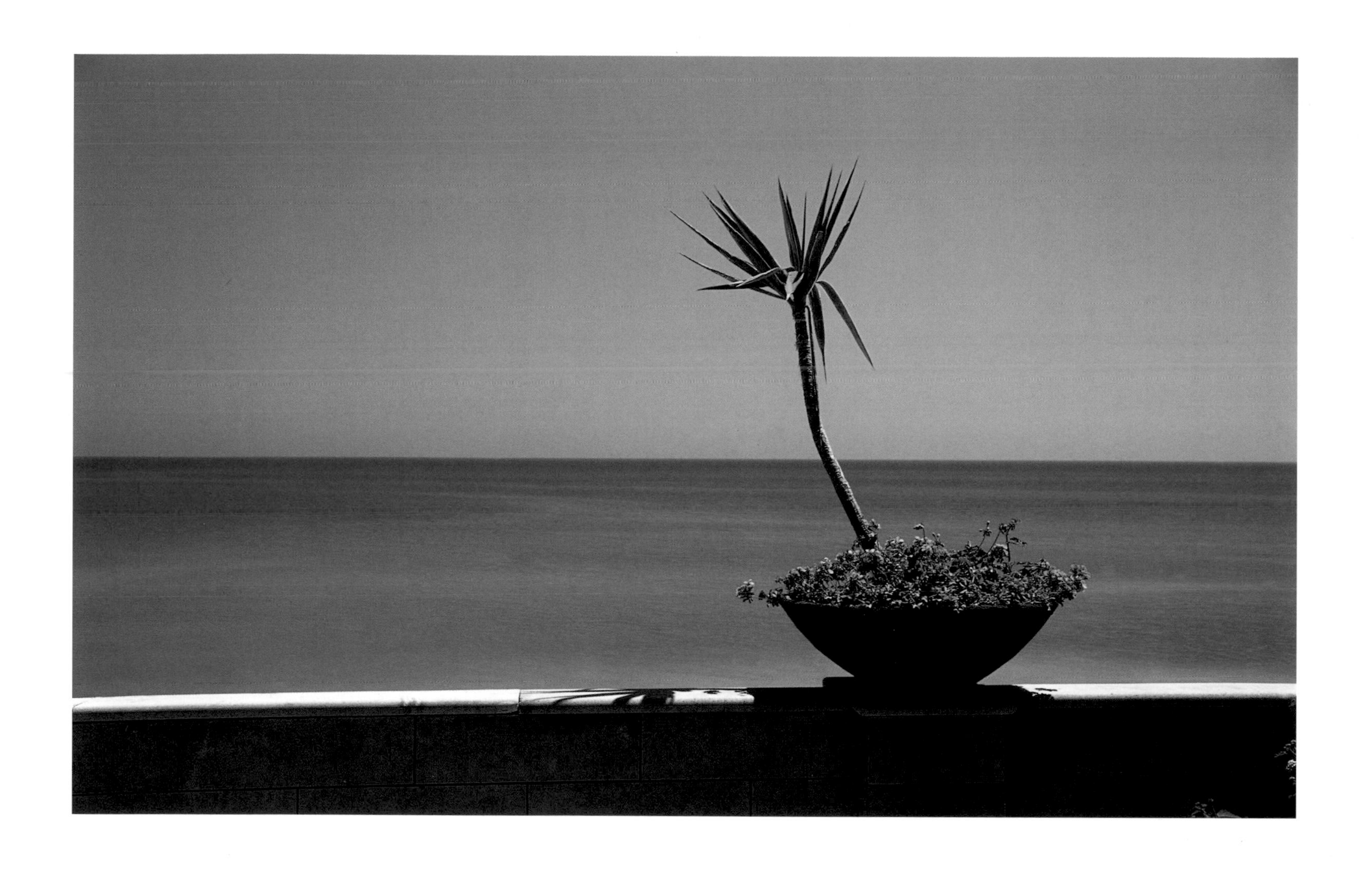

Flowers and shrubs are used ornamentally everywhere in Cyprus. This well-filled pot stands on a wall overlooking Pissouri Bay.
Opposite: The rooftops and towers of the Machairas Monastery, whose present buildings
date from the early 20th centuy. The monastery is set amongst the Troodos Mountains about 25 miles (40km) from Nicosia.

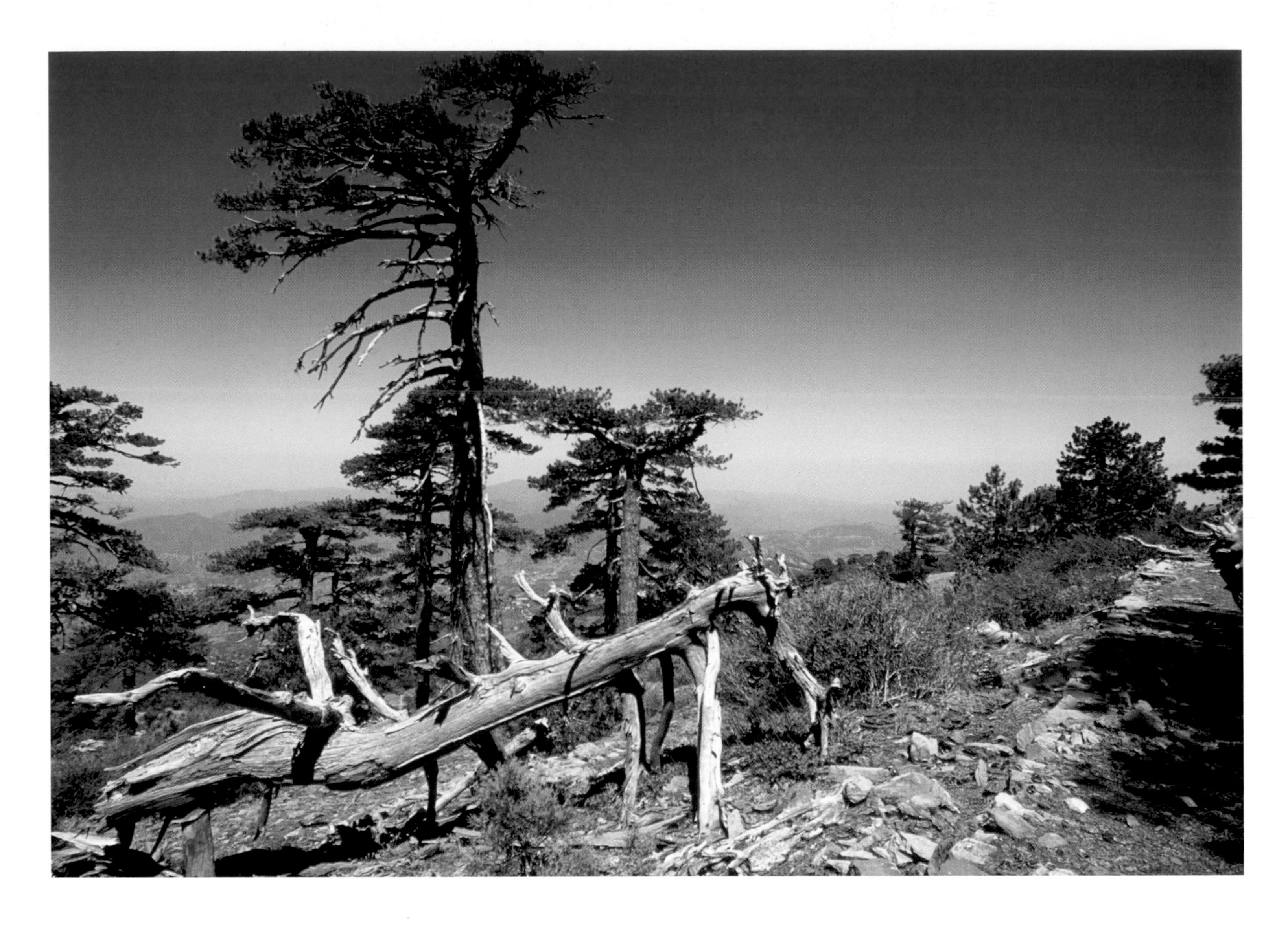

A fallen and dessicated tree trunk adds to the dramatic and rugged landscape of the Troodos Mountains, which dominate the entire southwest of the island.

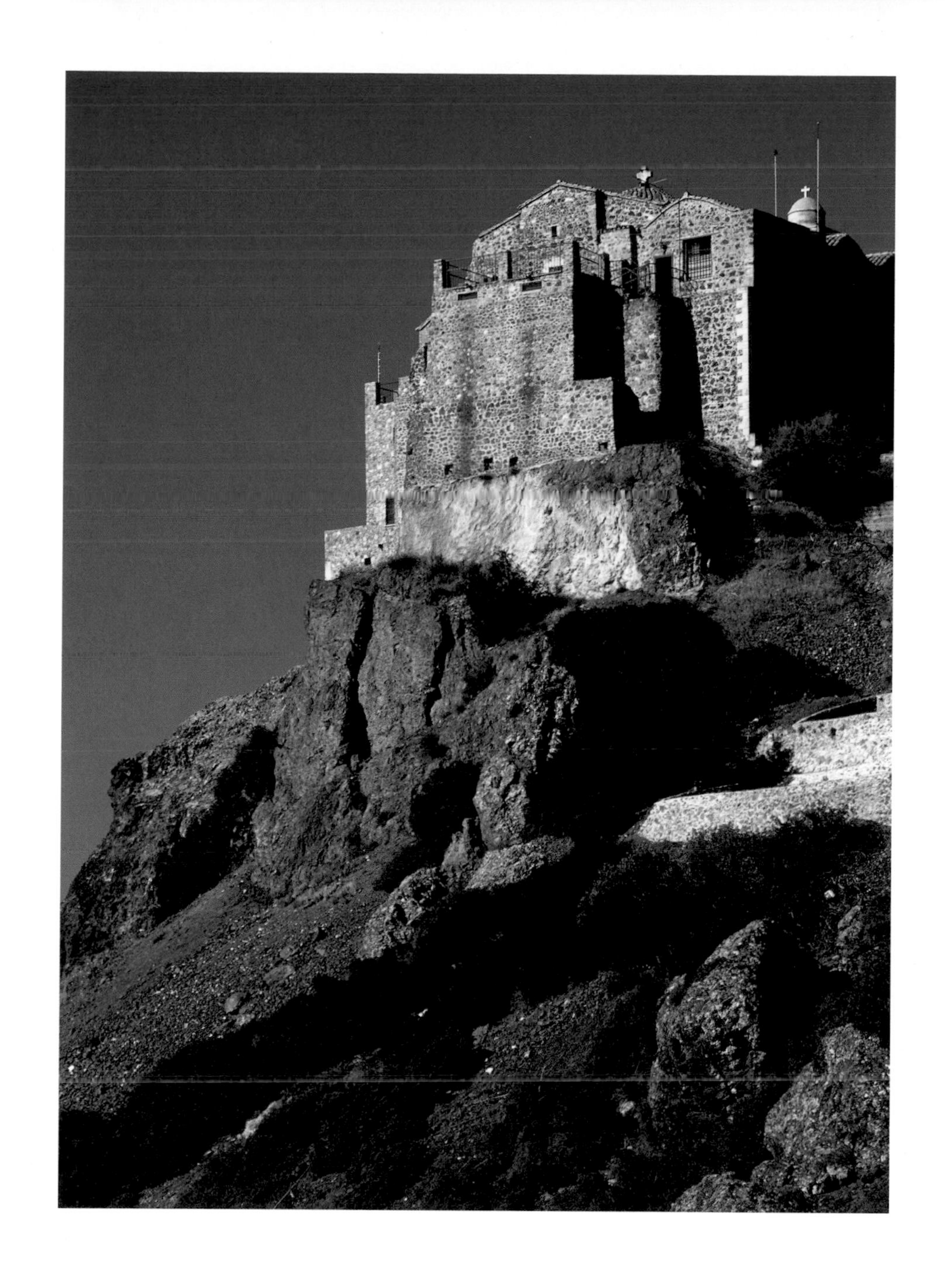

Stavrovouni Monastery, perched high above the countryside of Larnaka district.

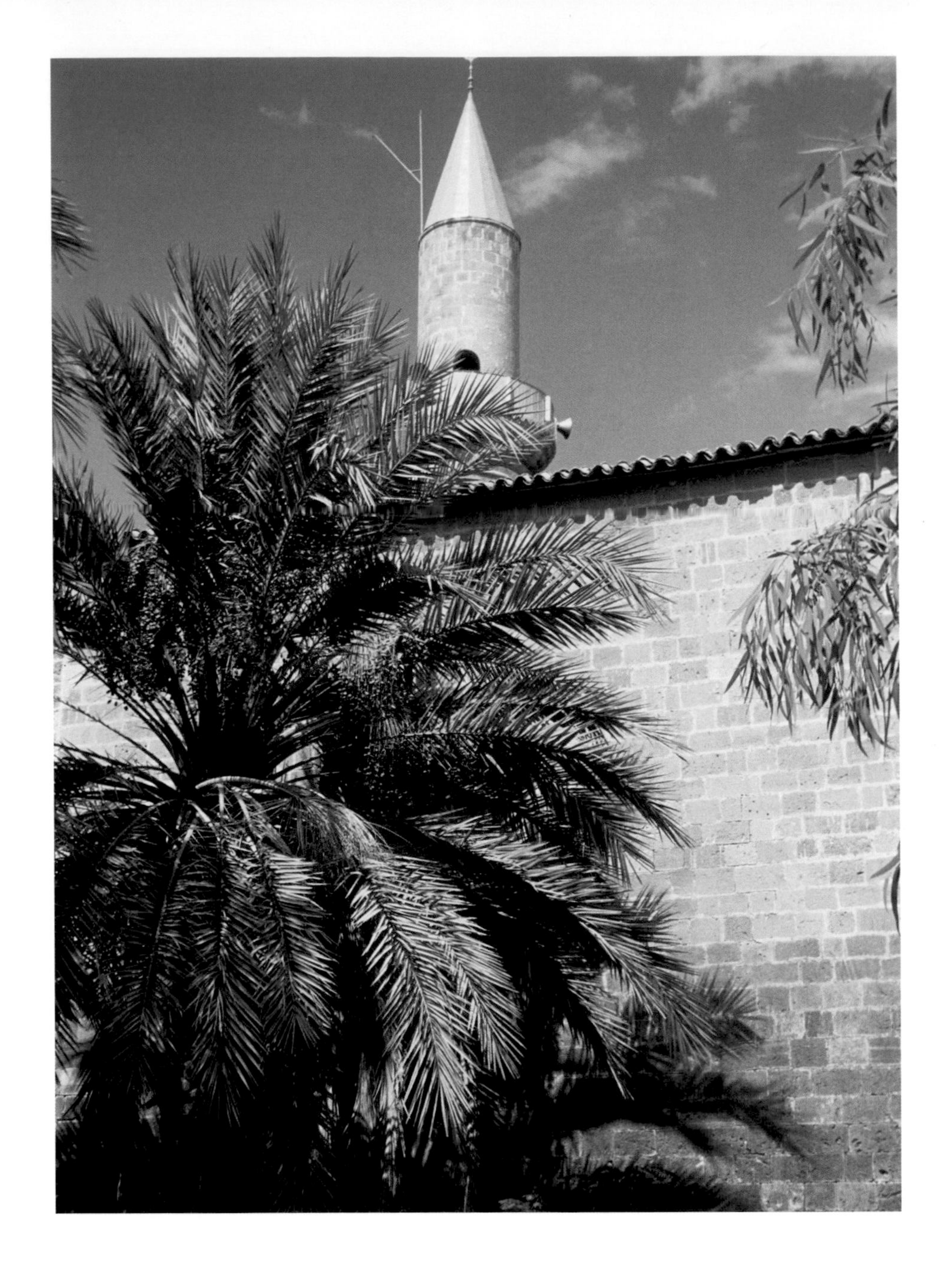

Almost hidden by the fronds of a large date palm, the tall minaret of the Ömeriye Mosque rises over Nicosia.

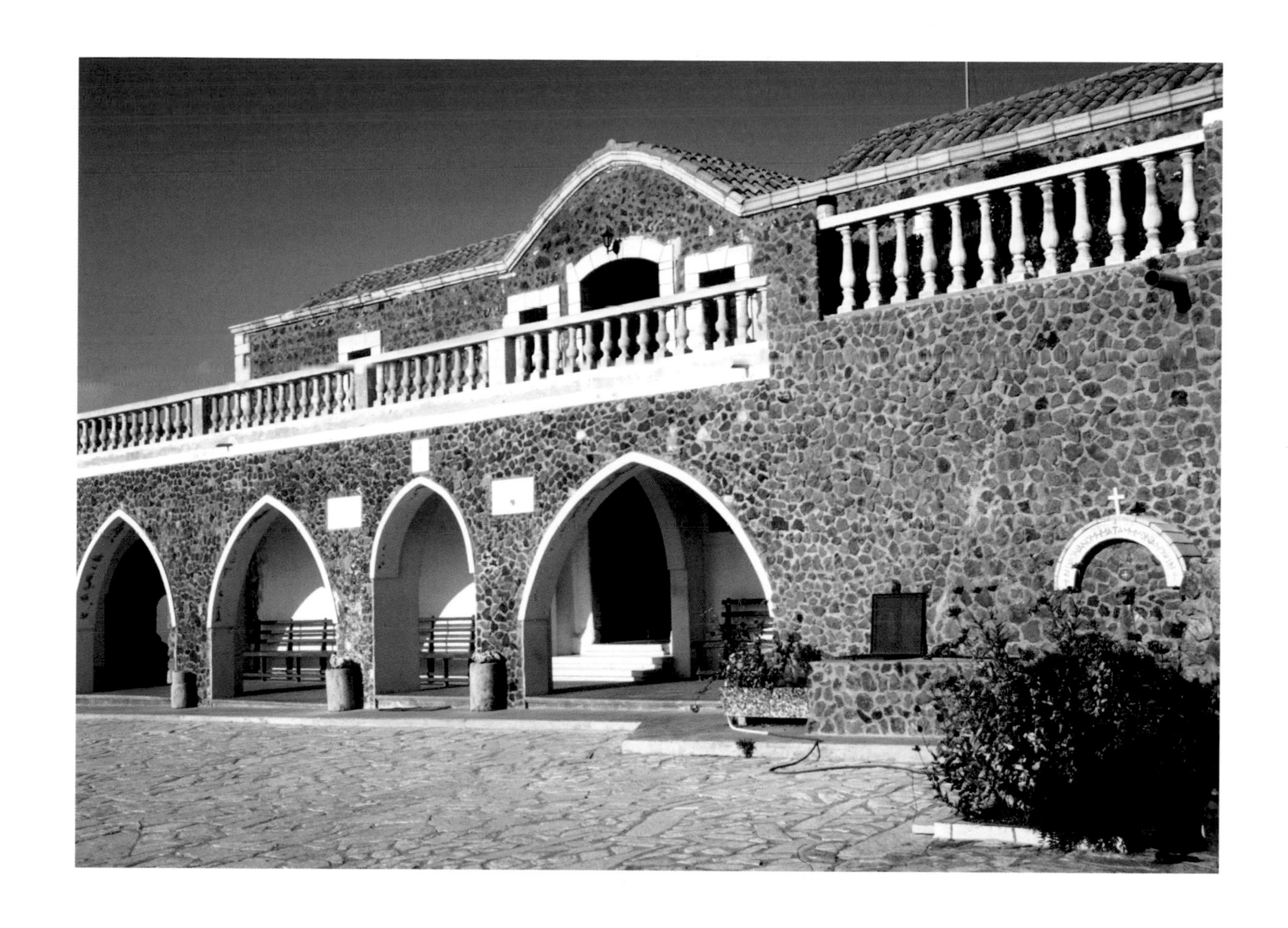

The 17th-century buildings of Stavrovouni Monastery, which was founded in AD 327.

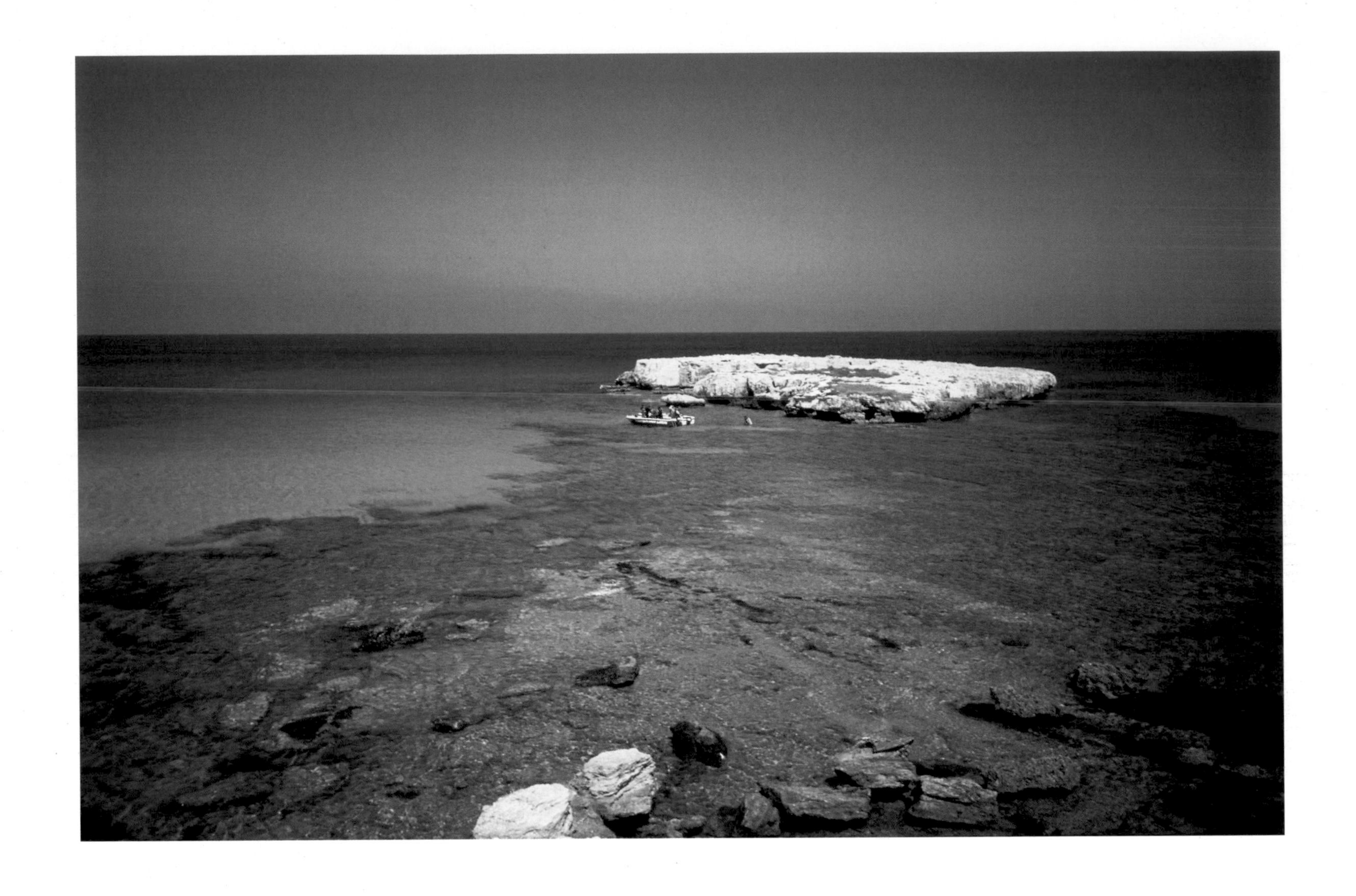

A group of holidaymakers enjoying the clear blue waters of the bay just offshore from Fontana Amoroza.
Opposite: The church in the centre of Pedoulas, a village in the Marathasa Valley of central Cyprus.

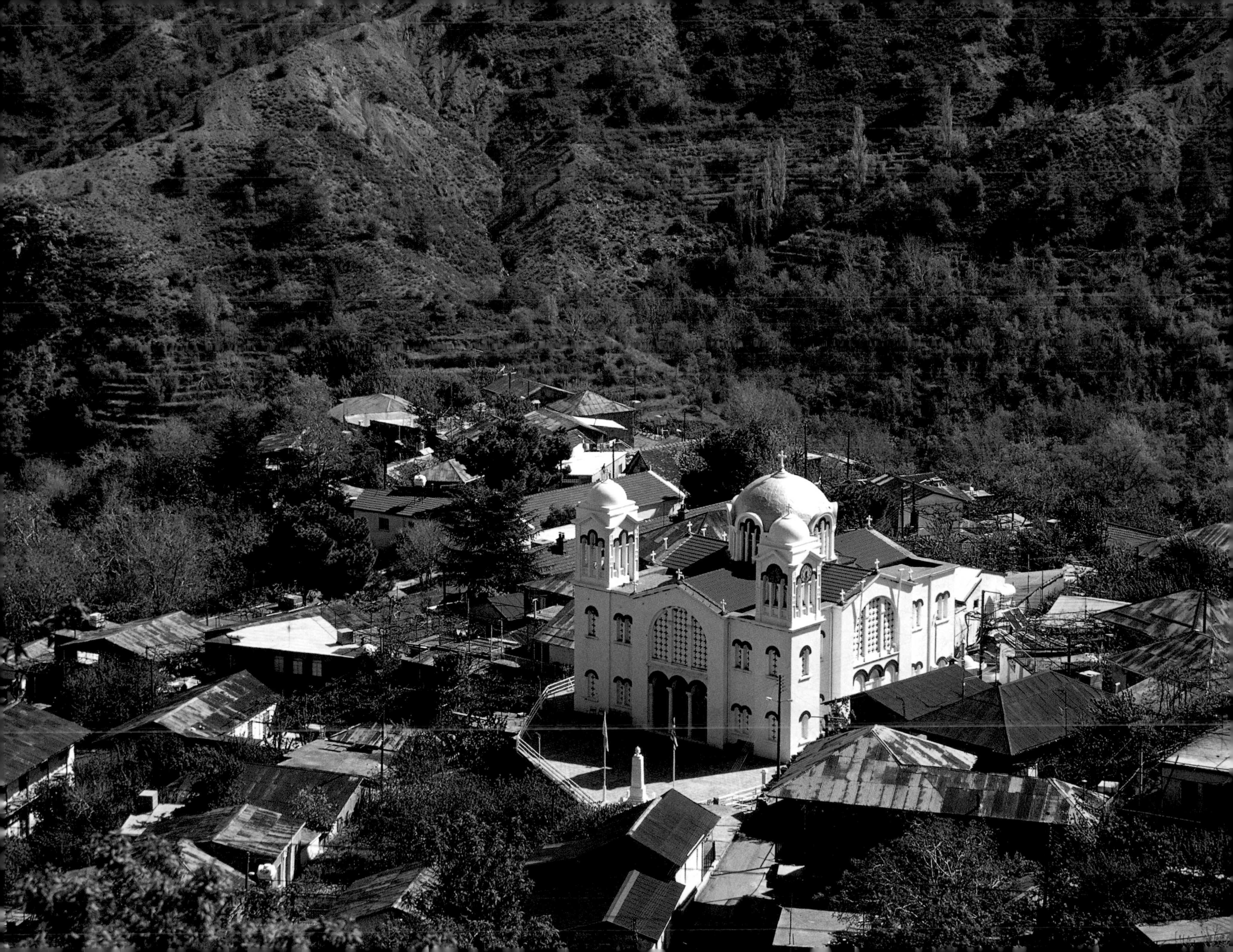

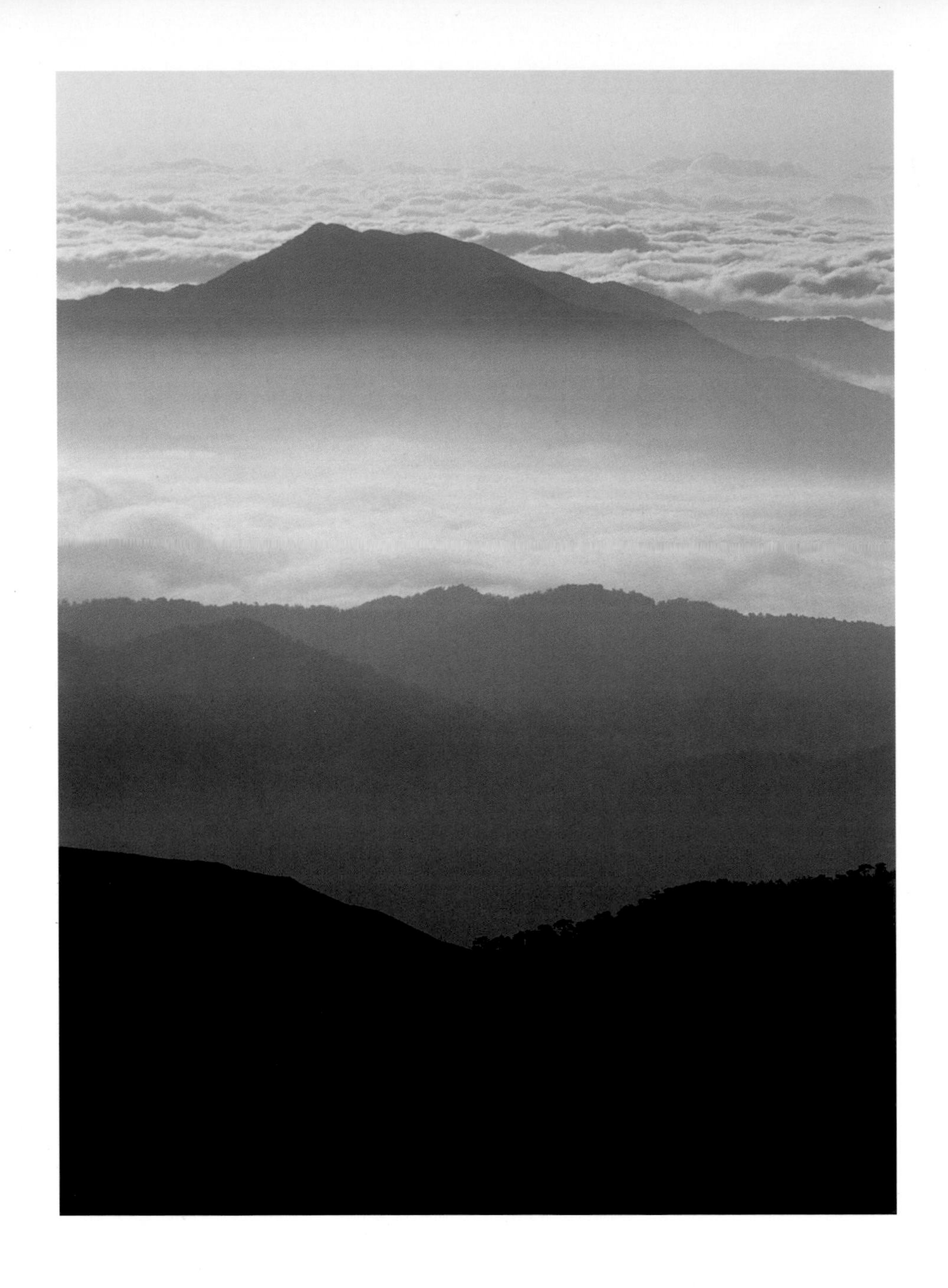

View east over Mount Olympos at dawn. This is the highest peak of the Troodos range.

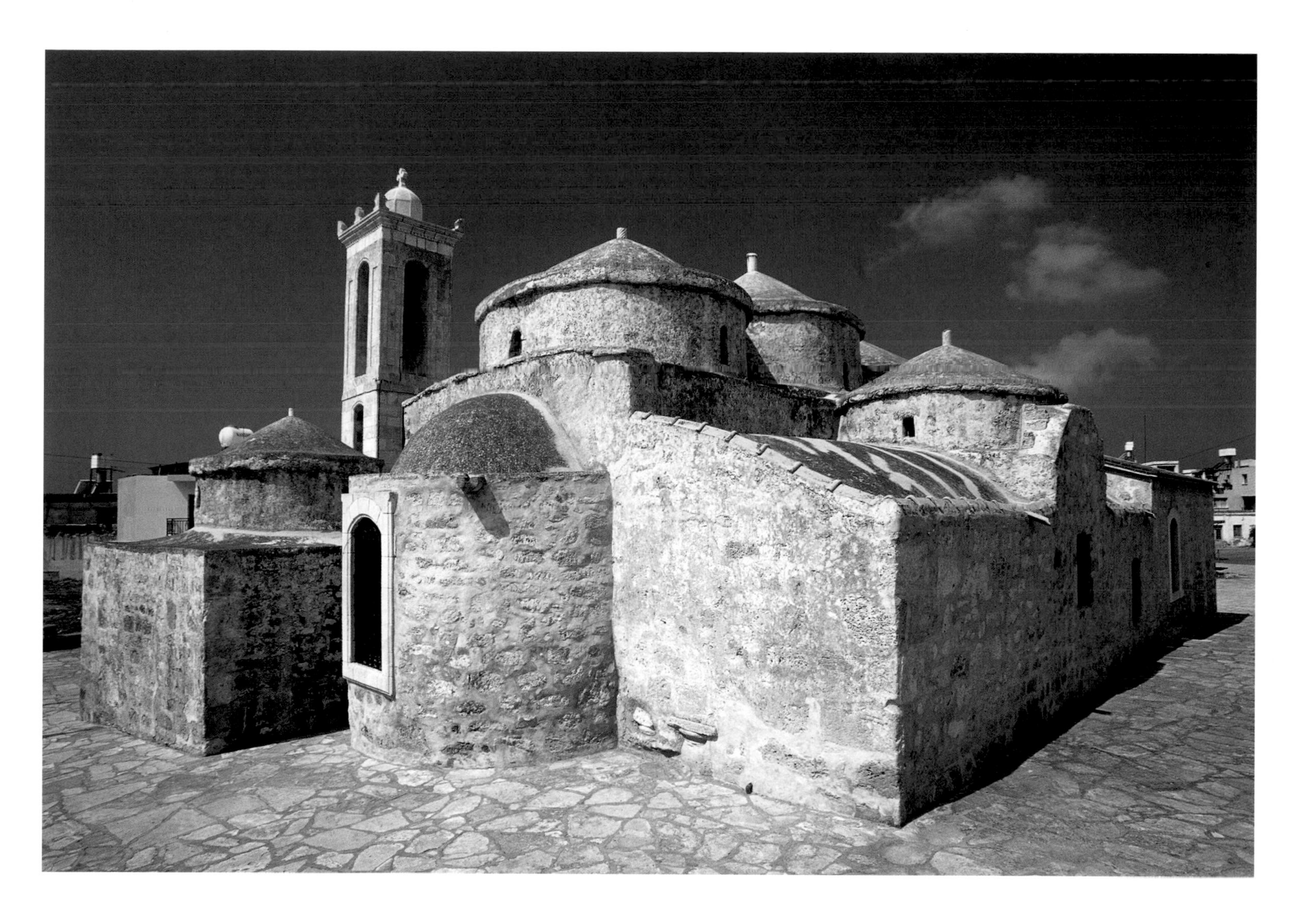

The five-domed church of Ayia Paraskevi in the village of Geroskipou, on the island's southwestern coast. The church was originally built in the 9th century.

INDEX